CANDLEHOLDERS

CREATIVE

Susan Kieffer found this piece of driftwood on a beach in the Florida Keys.

Much to her delight, she discovered that slender tapers fit the holes that the worms had so generously carved out.

CREATIVE
CANDLEHOLDERS
FROM ELEGANT TO WHIMSICAL

60
PROJECTS
TO SUIT
EVERY
STYLE

MORGENTHAL

LARK BOOKS

Art Director: Dana Irwin
Production: Dana Irwin and Hannes Charen
Assistant Editors: Heather Smith and Catharine Sutherland
Photography: Sandra Stambaugh

Library of Congress Cataloging-in-Publication Data

Morgenthal, Deborah, 1950-

     Creative candleholders : from elegant to whimsical, 60 projects to suit every style / Deborah Morgenthal. – 1st ed.

          p. cm.

       ISBN 1-57990-147-6 (paper)

      1. Handicraft. 2. Candlesticks. I. Title.

TT157.M69393 1999   99-20195

745.595'3–dc21   CIP

10 9 8 7 6 5 4 3 2 1

First Edition
Published by Lark Books
50 College St.
Asheville, NC 28801, US

Special thanks to Warren Fluharty for the use of his shop, Warren Fluharty Designs, location for the photograph on page 3.

Contents

INTRODUCTION

I am sure that there are still people living among us who buy a candle because it matches their couch, proudly display it on their coffee table, and never, ever light it. I also personally know people who burn candles only when the power goes out. And, hard though it is to believe, there are people who think that the function of a candleholder is to hold a candle in a stable and upright position to avoid setting their house on fire.

This book is not for people like these.

Yes, it's true that candlesticks started out as crude, functional objects in which to place a burning candle; but, then again, there was a time during the Middle Ages when common folk could not afford to buy beeswax candles. No wonder those times were called the Dark Ages.

Today, in growing numbers, people are buying candles in many shapes, sizes, colors, and aromas, simply because they love the way candlelight makes them feel—chasing away the blues, encouraging romance, setting the stage for a festive family dinner. For the true candle lover, there is no occasion that is not a perfect occasion for lighting a candle, and no room that is off-limits to its illuminating appeal, be it bathroom or living room.

This love of candles has translated into booming sales for companies and individuals who make and sell candles, as well as for the folks who market the raw materials for making your own candles at home. In fact, our book, *The Complete Candlemaker* by Norma Coney, published in 1997, continues to be one of our strongest sellers.

So it stands to reason that people who love to buy, make, and, most importantly, use candles, consider candleholders to be an integral part of the candle experience. They hunt out interesting candlesticks, votive holders, sconces, and other containers that possess artistic merit or simply look great—while still holding the candle in an upright position.

To be honest, great-looking candlesticks have been a tradition spanning centuries in many world cultures. Using gourds, wood, silver, gold, brass, glass, and clay, artisans have fashioned beautiful and functional candlesticks that reflect the motifs, symbols, and decorative style of the times in which they lived.

We have put this book together *in the spirit of that enduring tradition.*

We invited 26 talented designers to make candleholders that reflect their distinctive style. We encouraged them to use any kind of material and any kind of object. The result is a gorgeous and inspiring book featuring more than 60 projects you can make, plus many ideas for turning ordinary "stuff" into fantastic and functional candleholders.

Like to paint? Here's your chance to paint table legs, drain plungers, drinking glasses, terra-cotta pots, soda cans and bottles, wooden deck pieces, and dry gourds, and turn them into appealing candleholders.

Like woodworking? You can cut and assemble wood to construct attractive candlesticks and lanterns. *Attracted to flea markets?* You can give a whole new life to your collection of finds, from rubber stamp holders to standing ash trays. *Specialize in unusual containers?* We'll tell you how to melt wax, and then turn your favorite tea cup, tin can, or muffin tin into a container candle. *Enjoy winter holidays?* We'll help you celebrate Christmas, Hanukkah, or Kwanza with some terrific candelabras.

What's more, we'll show you how to *transform ordinary objects*—from red peppers to plumbing parts—into candleholders, simply by putting a candle in them.

We hope you find many candleholders in this book that will match your home decor and personal style. The projects are fun and easy to make. Our only warning: *This activity can become habit-forming.* We guarantee you will look at the world in a new way; no wormholed piece of driftwood, section of copper plumbing, or glass salt seller will be safe! See those egg shells left over from breakfast...those metal gears rusting in the backyard...that wooden plant stand...the take-out Chinese food container...

May visions of candleholders dance in your head and flickering candles light your way up to bed!

The following is a riddle from Victorian times...

> *Little Nannie Etticoat*
>
> *In a white petticoat*
>
> *and a red nose.*
>
> *The longer she stands,*
>
> *the shorter she grows.*
>
> *What is she?*

(a candle)

Above, multi-colored molded candles from Hemphill Candle Company; right, rolled beeswax candles from Illuminee Du Monde

Candles are available commercially in an amazing range of styles and colors. If you're interested in making your own candles, you can easily create dozens and dozens of attractive and distinctive candles. There are many books on the subject, including *The Complete Candlemaker* by Norma Coney (Lark Books, 1997).

A Few Words about Wax

Whether it's a freestanding pyramid-shaped candle or a hand-dipped multicolored taper, how a candle burns depends mostly on the wax used to make it. The two main types of wax used in candlemaking are beeswax and paraffin.

Beeswax is naturally produced from honeybee hives and is clean burning and sweet smelling. Beeswax candles have a cream or golden color and burn slowly. Beeswax candles can be hand-rolled from thin sheets, or the wax can be melted down and hand-dipped to make tapers or poured into molds. Rolled beeswax candles burn relatively quickly and tend to drip.

Paraffin is an inexpensive wax, derived from petroleum, and is widely used by today's candlemakers. It's clean burning and odorless, and has a glossy translucent finish. Available in bead, block, or pellet form, it's classified by melting points, broadly categorized as low (126 to 134°F/52°C to 57°C), medium (135 to 144°F/57°C to 62°C), and high (145 to 200°F/63°C to 93°C). Because paraffin is white, it can be blended with dye chips to produce any color. Paraffin wax drips a lot when used alone, so stearin is often added to the wax. Other additives are also used to raise its melting point, increase its hardness, and achieve a number of desired qualities for candlemaking.

Paraffin is also sold granulated into small beads (see the goblet on page 65). Bead wax comes in a variety of colors and scents, and can be mixed or layered to create colorful candles.

Candle Styles

Candles can be categorized into several main styles: Container candles, molded candles, hand-dipped or molded tapers, and specialty candles.

Container Candles

Container candles are very popular and offer another way to decorate your home. Melted wax can be poured into many types of containers, from paper-covered glasses to colorful tin cans to coconut shells. Paraffin wax with a low melting point makes the best container candles. For more information, see Making Container Candles on page 50.

Tapers

Tapers generally range in height from 6 inches (15 cm) to 18 inches (45 cm) and are of varying thicknesses. As their name implies, tapers are wider at the bottom and narrower at the tip. They are available in an assortment of styles and colors to match every occasion, and can be made from paraffin or beeswax that has been either hand-dipped or machine molded. Hand-dipped tapers are made by continually dipping a wick into melted wax until several layers have built up, so their sizes can vary depending on the length of wick and can occasionally be found smaller than 6 inches (15 cm) in height.

Beyond the prism of colors and range of sizes that apply to tapers, candlemakers also use a variety of techniques to create dazzling surface designs. You can find tapers that have been

Below, assorted hand-tipped tapers

dipped multiple times in different colored waxes to create complementary layers, and others that have been hand carved, painted, marbled, stenciled, adorned with wax appliqués, or twisted, to produce stunning creations. Many of the colored hand-dipped tapers sold commercially are created by overdipping a white taper into colored wax.

FLAT AND PEGGED

Like taper candles, flat and pegged candles are widely available in stores. They come in several colors, and are formed in molds to ensure their columnlike design. Some have a pegged bottom that makes for a smoother fit in many candleholders.

OTHER MOLDED CANDLES

Pillar, star pillar, pyramid, star taper, square, rectangular, round, oval—these are just some of the types of molded candles that are available. Candlemakers can use professional or homemade molds to form melted paraffin, beeswax,

Tealights embedded in fresh apples make a cheerful autumn centerpiece.

Opposite top, white molded candles from Guinevere's Candlemakers; opposite bottom, floral molded candles from Illuminee Du Monde

11

forewarned: these candles tend to burn unevenly and drip a lot as the wax melts at different rates around the candle.

TEALIGHTS

Tealights are tiny candles that sit in metal cups and are perfect for use in potpourri burners and in luminary containers. They are available in an ever-widening range of colors and fragrances, and tend to burn quickly.

VOTIVES

Every house has at least a few of these simple and inexpensive little candles. Votives are generally 2 inches (5 cm) in height and about 1½ inches (3.8 cm) in width, and are made by pouring melted wax into special mini-cup molds. They are available in a wide range of colors and fragrances, and can also be formed out of beeswax.

FLOATING CANDLES

These popular candles are molded and hand carved in beautiful shapes designed for floating in water in bowls, vases, bathtubs, or ponds. A cluster of lit candles adds a special glow to the water's surface. They range in size from 2 to 6 inches (5 to 15 cm) in diameter.

Above, Canton vase candles from Two's Company Inc.; opposite, chunk candles from Wax Wares

or a combination of waxes into freestanding candles. These can be found in a variety of colors, fragrances, and sizes, depending on the source. When using molds, other materials are often used: a mold sealer; a hardening agent, such as stearic acid; and a release agent, such as silicone or cooking spray, to keep the wax from sticking to the mold when it hardens. Although most molded candles can stand on their own, it's wise to use a candle-holder underneath them in case they drip.

CHUNK CANDLES

These great-looking molded candles are usually made from paraffin wax. While the wax is still liquid in the mold, the candlemaker embeds chunks of wax in different colors or in the same color as the molded candle. As the candle burns, the light bounces beautifully off these small chunks. Be

CHURCH OR ALTAR CANDLES

Church candles are traditionally white or cream colored, straight-sided candles that have been used in church ceremonies for centuries. Found in many sizes, from votives to slender tapers to imposing 15-inch-tall (37.5 cm) pillars, they are admired for their simplicity. Their design and color implies purity. Church candles burn slowly because they contain a high proportion of beeswax.

SPECIALTY CANDLES

Using a variety of techniques, candlemakers can produce candles that will make you hesitate before you light the match. You can find candles embedded with dried fruit or flowers, others that look tie-dyed, even candles "frosted" with whipped wax—the list is endless! Specially shaped molds are used to make candles that simulate real objects, such as fruit, teapots, birthday cakes—even Greek sculpture. Almost any plain candle can be surface decorated with paint, natural materials, stencils, glitter, beads, or anything else that will stick to the wax.

WOOD & PAINTED WOOD.

SWIVEL TAPER HOLDERS

The rounded edges of this elegant candleholder give it the classic look of Danish furniture. This project is not only easy to make, but a cinch to store in a drawer until the perfect occasion arises.

DESIGNER
ROBIN CLARK

WHAT YOU NEED

1 piece of cedar, 5½ x 7 x 1 inches
   (13.8 x 17.5 x 2.5cm)

1 dowel, 5 x ¼ inches
   (12.5 x .6 cm)

Pencil

Sandpaper

Clear stain

Paintbrush

4 tapers, 1 inch (2.5 cm) wide

Drill with ¼- and ½-inch (.6 and 1.3 cm) bits

Band saw (or scroll saw)

Router with ¼-inch (.6 cm) roundover bit
   (or sandpaper)

WHAT YOU DO

1

Stand the rectangular block of wood on its 1-inch (2.5 cm) wide edge so that it's 5½ inches (13.8 cm) tall and 7 inches (17.5 cm) long. On the top edge, mark a point 1 inch (2.5 cm) from one end of the block, centered. Drill a hole at this point ¼ inch (.6 cm) wide and 5 inches (12.5 cm) deep.

2

Lay the rectangle down, flat on one side. Draw three lines, 1¼ inches (3 cm) apart, running parallel to the top of the block. Then, starting from the side of the block without the drilled hole, draw three lines, 1¼ inches (3 cm) apart, running parallel to the side of the block. Draw a curve at the corner at each intersection of the lines, and at the corner of the block without the hole. Use a band saw to cut these lines. Round over the edges.

3

You should now have four separate pieces of curved wood to work with. At the top of each curve, drill a ½-inch (1.3 cm) hole about ½ inch (1.3 cm) deep. These holes will hold the candles.

4

Sand and stain all the pieces, and let dry.

5

Finally, arrange the four pieces so that they form a rectangle again, and insert the 5-inch-long (12.5 cm) dowel into the ¼-inch (.6 cm) hole. Once you stand it up, the dowel will hold the structure together and allow the pieces to pivot.

FIESTA CANDLESTICKS

Great colors and simple brush strokes can dramatically transform plain wooden candlesticks. Here the designer used different color combinations to create two distinctive pairs of candleholders.

DESIGNER
TRACY PAGE STILWELL

WHAT YOU NEED

Fine-grade sandpaper

White acrylic primer

¼-inch (.6 cm) and ½-inch (1.3 cm) paintbrushes, including medium flat, narrow flat, and medium round

Rags

Clear acrylic spray

Tapers or flat candles

FOR MULTICOLORED CANDLESTICKS:

Acrylic paints: white, black, dark blue, medium blue, light blue, yellow-green, dark green, yellow, orange, medium pink, purple

Pair of wooden candlesticks, 7 inches tall (17.5 cm)*

*sold in craft-supply stores

FOR BLACK AND WHITE CANDLESTICKS:

Pair of wooden candlesticks, 2¼ inches tall (6 cm)*

¼-inch (.6 cm) angle paintbrush

*sold in craft-supply stores

WHAT YOU DO

1

Sand each candlestick.

2

Apply the white base coat over the entire piece and let dry. You may want to sand lightly after the base coat has dried.

MULTI-COLORED CANDLESTICKS

3

Starting at the bottom, apply the dark blue to the first

round, medium blue to the second round, and light blue to the next. Apply the yellow-green next, followed by yellow, pink, and purple. Paint the top with one or more coats of white. Let it dry.

4

Again, starting at the bottom, use the dark green to make lines around the bottom ring. Use the point of a round brush to make the small yellow dots on the medium blue and purple rings.

5

Paint over the yellow section with watered-down orange paint to create a glazed effect. Work in small sections, and use the rag to pat off most of the orange paint; the yellow should show through the orange.

6

Add white paint to the pink to make the color for the light stripe around the pink section. Use the narrow flat brush to apply the stripes.

7

To create the small orange squares on the yellow section, dip a tiny piece of sponge into the orange paint, or use a small narrow brush.

8

Use the narrow flat brush to make the black lines around the top.

9

Finish the top by painting the inside black.

10

When the candlesticks are dry, spray them with clear acrylic to protect the surface of the paint.

BLACK AND WHITE CANDLESTICKS

11

Follow steps 1 and 2.

12

Apply another coat of white paint over the top half of one stick and over the bottom half of the other.

13

Apply the black paint to the other portion of each candlestick. You may have to cover

the area two or three times to get complete coverage.

14

Use a narrow flat brush to make white stripes on the black base. Make the black spaces about the same size as your white brush strokes. Dots can be made with the tip of the round brush. Use the tip of the round brush to make angled lines around the top of the stick, as well as the dots at the end of each line. Use the narrow flat brush to make the strokes on the white base, creating a checkerboard effect. Make the white spaces the same size as your black strokes. The white triangles can be made with the narrow flat brush. Use the point of the round brush to make small dots at the corners of the triangles. The heart shapes at the top are made with two strokes of the angle brush.

15

Repeat steps 9 and 10.

Designer Rob Pulleyn sawed a newel post into sections, and then glued a dried ginkgo leaf to each one to create this stunning trio.

FLEA-MARKET SPECIAL

The designer used colorful acrylic paints to turn a stodgy old ashtray stand into an eye-catching candlestick. Let the shape of your stand guide the way in which you decorate it.

DESIGNER
TRACY PAGE STILWELL

WHAT YOU NEED

Wooden ashtray stand

Fine-grade sandpaper

Paintbrushes, ½ and 1 inch (1.3 and 2.5 cm) wide, including flat and round-tip

White acrylic primer

Acrylic paints: white, black, light blue, dark blue, dark green, yellow, lime, apple green, and turquoise

Rags

Gold permanent marker

Clear acrylic spray

Large pillar candle

WHAT YOU DO

1

Sand the ashtray stand to remove old paint or wood stain.

2

Apply a white base coat over the entire piece, and let dry.

3

Lightly sand the ashtray stand again.

4

Starting at the base, apply a coat of white acrylic paint to those sections that will remain white.

5

Paint the stand in a pattern that works best with your particular ashtray stand.

6

To achieve the look of a cloud-filled blue sky, water down the light blue paint, apply it over the area, and then use the rag to pat off the excess.

7

Allow the stand to dry thoroughly.

8

Apply a second coat to the dark green and dark blue sections to create a rick look. Let dry.

9

Thin some black paint and add a layer on top of the dark green and dark blue sections. Apply the black paint to small sections, and wipe with a rag to remove some of the black paint.

10

Use a wide flat brush to make black stripes along the white base and anywhere else you want. Make black dots with the tip of a round brush.

11

Use the gold marker to create stars on the dark blue sections.

12

When the stand is completely dry, spray it with clear acrylic to protect the finish.

WOODEN DECKING CANDLESTICKS

These imposing candlesticks are very simple to make. Because you use treated decking lumber, they can be left outdoors to age nicely in the elements, or used indoors, where they're sure to attract praise and attention.

DESIGNER
ROB PULLEYN

WHAT YOU NEED

Assorted deck rails and decorative decking details*

Sandpaper

Water-based wood stain in blue or light green

Paintbrush

Several large pillar or altar candles

Saw

*available at building-supply outlets

WHAT YOU DO

1

Cut the deck rails into several lengths. You may need to saw off some rounded sides so that you wind up with two flat sides.

2

Sand any rough edges.

3

Mix the colored wood stain with water so that you wind up with a very diluted tint. Apply three coats of stain, letting each coat dry. Used on treated lumber like this, which often has a blue or green color, the stain creates an appealing, weather-worn patina.

OUTDOOR LANTERNS

These handsome red cedar lanterns are perfect for illuminating a deck or patio. The clever design makes lighting the candles a real breeze while preventing a breeze from blowing them out.

DESIGNER:
ROBIN CLARK

WHAT YOU NEED

(for one lantern)

3 feet (10 m) western red cedar or other outdoor wood, 8 inches wide, 1 inch thick (20 x 2.5 cm)

1 dowel, 11 inches (28 cm) long, $\frac{3}{8}$ inch (.9 cm) wide

4 deck screws, $1\frac{1}{2}$ inch (3.8 cm) long, #6 coarse thread

8 deck screws, 2 inches (5 cm) long, #8 coarse thread

4 pieces of $\frac{1}{8}$-inch-thick (.3 cm) tinted acrylic plastic mea suring $5\frac{1}{2}$ x 8 inches (13.8 x 20 cm)

Wood glue

Sandpaper

Paintbrushes

Clear finish

Pillar candle, 2 inches (5 cm) wide, 6 inches (15 cm) tall

Table saw

Drill with $\frac{1}{8}$-, $\frac{3}{8}$-, 2- and 3-inch (.3-, .9-, 5-, 7.5-cm) bits

Screwdriver

Band saw (or similar tool) for rounding corners

Router with $\frac{1}{4}$-inch (.6 cm) round-over bit

WHAT YOU DO

1

Cut the cedar into eight pieces with the following dimensions:

2 pieces measuring $7\frac{1}{4}$ x $7\frac{1}{4}$ inches (18 x 18 cm)

2 pieces measuring 5 x 5 inches (12.5 x 12.5 cm)

4 pieces measuring 1 x 1 x 8 inches (2.5 x 2.5 x 20 cm)

2

Drill a $\frac{1}{8}$-inch (.3 cm) pilot hole $\frac{3}{4}$ inches (1.9 cm) in from each corner of the two large squares and in one of the 5-inch square blocks. In one of the large squares, drill a 3-inch (7.5 cm) diameter hole through the center of the board. Drill a 2-inch (5 cm) diameter hole through half the depth of one of the 5-inch (12.5 cm) square blocks.

3

Use the four $1\frac{1}{2}$ inch (3.8 cm) screws to attach the remaining 5-inch (12.5 cm) square block (without the hole), centered, to the bottom of the remaining large square (without the hole).

4

Center the 5-inch (12.5 cm) square (with the hole) on top of the large square without the hole. Drill a $\frac{3}{8}$-inch (.9 cm) hole 1 inch (2.5 cm) in from one corner of the 5-inch (12.5 cm) square block. Then drill a corresponding hole in the large block that will form the lid of the lantern; the dowel will pass through the top of the lantern and into the 5-inch (12.5 cm) square block resting inside.

5

Use the band saw to round the

the hole and hold a moment until the glue sets up.

7

Set the table saw so that the blade is exposed $\frac{1}{4}$ inch (.6 cm) and the fence is $\frac{5}{8}$ inch (1.6 cm) from the blade. Run the posts through to cut a groove in two sides of each post, one positioned $\frac{1}{2}$ inch (1.3 cm) from the inside corner and one $\frac{1}{4}$ inch (.6 cm) from the outside corner.

8

Use the drill and screwdriver to attach the posts to the bottom large square with four of the 2-inch (5 cm) screws.

9

Round over all the exposed edges and sand any rough areas.

10

Apply a coat of clear finish to all the wood parts.

11

Once the wood has dried, slide the acrylic plastic sheets into the grooves in the posts.

12

Put the dowel assembly in the lantern base, and slip the top over the dowel. Use the drill to attach the top to the posts with the remaining 2-inch (5 cm) screws.

corners of the small square, then round over all of the edges of the lantern and the four post pieces.

6.

Put a small dab of glue in the $\frac{3}{8}$-inch (.9 cm) corner hole drilled in the 5-inch (12.5 cm) square block (see the detail photo). Insert the dowel into

26

Loi Krathong

Once the sun has set and the full moon of mid-November begins to cast its milky glow over the fields of Thailand, the country's rivers and waterways come alive with lights of their own. The majestic glow on the water comes from fleets of small, lotus-shaped boats fashioned from banana leaves and paper that fill the waterways. Each boat bears a lighted candle, a flower, joss sticks (a type of incense), and a tiny coin. The vessels have been launched by celebrants of Loi Krathong, an ancient Thai holiday often deemed the loveliest of the country's festivals.

Several stories vie for the true origin of Loi ("to float") Krathong ("leaf cup" or "bowl"), the first being the legend of King Ramakhamhaeng's pilgrimage. According to the tale, while the king was performing a pilgrimage from temple to temple along the river, one of his wives devised a way to please him and Lord Buddha simultaneously. She created a paper lantern resembling a lotus flower, the symbol of the human spirit, and set it afloat on the river bearing a lighted candle. The king was so delighted by this act that he ordered all subjects to perform similar boat launches on a designated night every year.

Others trace the holiday to the ancient practice of giving thanks to Me Khongkha, the Mother of Water, to wash away the

sins of the past year. In the context of this tradition, the coins are a means of asking forgiveness for thoughtless ways during the year. Finally, Loi Krathong may serve to commemorate the lotus blossoms that are said to have sprung up beneath the Lord Buddha's feet when he took his first baby steps.

No matter where the true origin of Loi Krathong lies, this magical celebration of candlelight remains one of the world's most unique and beautiful winter festivals.

Photos courtesy of the Tourism Authority of Thailand, New York Office

PALACE CANDLESTICKS

These two painted candlesticks have a regal and playful style, reminiscent of the Queen of Heart's palace in Alice in Wonderland. They would look right at home in your "palace," too.

DESIGNER
SHEILA ENNIS

WHAT YOU NEED

(for each candlestick)

Wooden table leg*

Wooden base*

Taper or column candle

Sandpaper

Paintbrushes

Electric drill with ⅞- or 1-inch (2.2 or 2.5 cm) wood-boring bit

FOR BLACK AND GOLD CANDLESTICK:

Black acrylic paint

Gold leaf paint**

Gold leaf pen**

FOR PURPLE AND RED CANDLESTICK:

2 wooden drawer pulls

Carpenter's glue

Purple and red acrylic paint

Raw umber tint**

*sold at home improvement stores

**sold at art-supply stores

WHAT YOU DO

1

The top of the table leg, which you will use as the bottom of the candlestick, comes with a screw. Drill a starter hole in the wooden base and attach the top of the table leg to the base with the screw.

2

Drill a hole in the top of the candlestick large enough to fit your candle.

3

Sand the candlestick.

BLACK AND GOLD CANDLESTICK

4

Paint the candlestick black and let dry.

5

Highlight the edges with gold leaf paint. Use the gold leaf pen to make the crosshatch designs where desired.

PURPLE AND RED CANDLESTICK

6

Paint the candlestick purple and red in a fashion that works with the shape of the table leg; then let dry.

7

Paint the drawer pulls red and let dry.

8

Glue the drawer pulls to the base.

9

Make a glaze with the raw umber tint and paint over the red areas, except for the drawer pulls. Let dry.

10

Sand down the finished piece to make it look aged.

Art director Dana Irwin made great use of a beautiful tree stump in her backyard. She hammered long finishing nails into the stump to serve as stakes for an assortment of altar, pillar, and votive candles.

METAL PIPES PARTS & WIRE.

Designer Rob Pulleyn discovered that metal plumbing connectors make elegant candlesticks. If you need to make the opening smaller, put a brass candle cup in each of the connectors.

Candlesticks by the Pound

With a discerning eye and a little elbow grease, designer Pat Scheible transformed discarded metal parts into distinctive candleholders.

DESIGNER:
PAT SCHEIBLE

What You Need

Metal machinery parts from salvage yard

Soft rags

Metal polish

Soft-bristle toothbrush

Paintbrushes

Patinating solutions*

Silicone solution

Assorted candles

*available at craft-supply stores

What You Do

1

If you've never visited your local metal salvage yard, you're in for a treat! Wear sturdy shoes and work gloves to protect yourself when you scrounge around. Look for interesting shapes.

Metals are sold by the pound, depending on their composition and the market demand. The designer purchased this stunning machine gear for just a few dollars.

2

Use rags to wipe off any grease.

3

Polish the metals with the toothbrush and a clean rag. The smooth finish of the gear polished well, so the designer simply left it alone. The pebbled finish of the plumbing parts did less well, so the designer painted on a patinating solution.

4

To maintain the sheen of the metal, cover the shiny areas of the metal with a light coating of a silicone solution.

COPPER WIRE CANDLEHOLDERS

Once you get the hang of bending copper wire into coils, the candle-holder possibilities are endless! Using the same technique and material the designer created three distinctive styles.

DESIGNER:
MARGARET DAHM

WHAT YOU NEED

#6 bare copper electrical wire*

Ball candle
(dripless, if possible)

Tall taper candles

Flat-nose pliers

Needle-nose pliers with
cutting edge

*available at electrical-supply
outlets; sold in 20-foot
(6 cm) coils

WHAT YOU DO

CANDLE BALL SCONCE

1

To make the reflector portion of the sconce, start with the whole coil of #6 copper wire and grab the tip of the loose end with the flat-nose pliers. Bend the wire around the pliers in an even, circular shape about ¾ to 1 inch (1.9 to 2.5 cm) in diameter (this is as small a circle as you can make with this wire). Using the pliers to grasp as you go, bend the wire around and around this circular shape in a flat, expanding spiral.

2

After bending two or three rows, stop using the pliers and bend the wire by hand. Bending by hand may seem a bit harder, but it will be easier to control the wire and will leave fewer plier teeth marks on the finished piece.

3.

Once your spiral reaches about 5 inches (12.5 cm) in diameter, you're ready to make the part of the sconce that holds the candle. Hold your reflector with the initial wire end (now in the center of the spiral) curving downward (this will make it easier to hang once completed) and bend the wire around the last lap of the reflector. Then bend the wire down, across the front of the reflector, and forward, forming a loose circle at least 2 inches (5 cm) in diameter and perpendicular to the reflector.

4

Pick a spot on the coil of wire that is 14 to 18 inches (35 to 45 cm) from the new 2-inch (5 cm) circle. Grasp the wire tightly at this point with the cutting edges of the needle-nose pliers, and spin the pliers around to score the wire as deeply as possible. Using the flat-nose pliers, grab as close to the scored line as possible and bend the wire tightly back and forth until it breaks.

5

Starting at your newly cut end, begin to make a flat spiral just as you did for the reflector. This spiral needs to be perpendicular to the reflector spiral and will form the bottom of the candleholder to cradle the ball candle. The twisting may be harder to control as you get closer to your 2-inch (5 cm) circle, so go slowly.

6

When this last spiral is positioned beneath the 2-inch (5 cm) circle, push the center of the spiral down to form the shape of the ball candle. The 2-inch (5 cm) circle of wire should be slightly larger than the candle and will form a railing to keep the candle in place.

COILED SPRING CANDLEHOLDER

6

Start with the whole coil of #6 copper wire, grabbing the loose end with the flat-nose pliers. Bend the wire around the pliers in an even, circular shape about 1 inch (2.5 cm) in diameter. TIP: You're making the uppermost part of the candleholder that will hold the candle, so test the diameter of your candle here to make sure it will fit.

7

Coil the wire tightly at a consistent diameter until it is about 2 inches (5 cm) tall.

8

Begin gradually widening both the diameter of the coils and the distance between each coil. Keep in mind that the finished candleholder should be about 5 inches (12.5 cm) tall with a diameter of about 4 inches (10 cm).

9

Follow step 4 to cut the wire.

10

After cutting the wire, bend by hand; start guiding each new coil beside the preceding coil, rather than underneath it, to widen the base of the candleholder. The wider the base, the more stable the structure will be.

11

Continue making coils until you have used up your length of cut wire. Remember that the taller the candleholder is, the more springy it will be. Although it may look appealing, a jiggling base is not an entirely desirable trait to have in a candleholder, so avoid skyscraper look-alikes!

DOUBLE-SPRING CANDELABRA

12

Begin this project like the others, taking the loose end of the whole coil of wire in the flat-nose pliers to form an even, circular shape about 1 inch (2.5 cm) in diameter. Test the diameter of your candle to make sure it will fit snugly.

13

Keep forming consistent, tight coils until you have a spring that stands about 1 inch (2.5

cm) tall. A good way to make tight coils is to use the pliers to grasp the wire and your other hand to bend the wire. Refer to each preceding coil as a guide to shape and size.

14

Once your spring reaches 1 inch (2.5 cm) in height, sweep the last coil away from the base of the spring as if you're making the top of a question mark, and follow through with a nice curved body heading toward the center of the candleholder. The question mark should measure about 3 inches (7.5 cm) long from top to bottom, with about 1½ inches (3.8 cm) separating the spring shape from the next section, the center spring.

15

Using the flat-nose pliers, grasp the wire firmly at the end of the question-mark shape. Bend it upright and curve it around to make a small circle that is perpendicular to the first spring. Keep bending the wire into coils, gradually widening the diameter as you go, and leaving a ¼-inch (.6 cm) space between each coil.

16

Once you reach a coil that looks about twice the size of the first coil in the center spring, start gradually reducing the coil size evenly until the two sides match.

17

Stretch out and curve the wire from the last coil of the center spring to form another question mark on this side. From the top of the question mark, bend the wire into a tight coil and continue coiling to form a spring shape that mirrors the spring on the opposite side. Be sure to test the candle to make sure it fits in this candleholder as well.

TIP: Refer to The Verdigris Process on page 37 for additional materials and instructions if you wish to apply verdigris (green-blue) tints to your copper projects.

The Verdigris Process

Aged copper that has a blue-green tint has become popular and desirable in recent years. This colorful coating, known as verdigris, forms naturally on brass, bronze, and copper over time as a result of chemical reactions. When it comes to home decorating, many people prefer to speed up nature's pace and start out with the look of exquisitely aged copper.

WHAT YOU NEED

Nonmetal container large enough to hold copper pieces

Wood shavings, shredded soft paper, and/or cat litter

Glass jar for mixing chemicals

Ammonia

Salt

Vinegar

Rubber gloves

Old towel

WHAT YOU DO

IMPORTANT NOTE: Vinegar and especially ammonia are extremely caustic if they come into contact with open cuts. Ammonia can be harmful to breathe if you're working in poorly ventilated areas. Be sure to work in a well-ventilated area and wear protective gloves.

1

In the container, assemble any combination of wood shavings, shredded soft paper, or cat litter.

2

To achieve a blue finish, pour ammonia into the jar, followed by a generous sprinkling of salt. To achieve a green finish, pour vinegar into the jar and mix with salt. Moisten (do not soak) the dry materials with the mixture you're using.

3

Place the copper pieces into the mixture, and cover the container loosely with the towel. The process will take a few days. TIP: Be sure to aerate the copper by occasionally turning the pieces during this time; the verdigris finish is caused by oxidation and, therefore, requires oxygen to work.

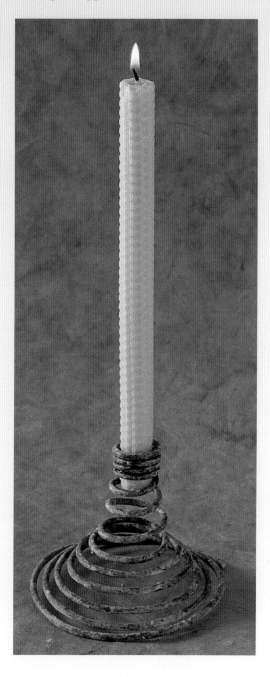

Art director Dana Irwin had the bright idea of pounding ordinary metal pipes into the ground at a friend's garden to create this collection of sturdy and imposing torches.

Pamela Brown successfully transformed two old copper lamps into gleaming candleholders, using copper polish and two new hurricane globes.

39

LEAD PIPE CANDLESTICKS

You can't get more industrial-chic than this handsome pair. Using off-the-shelf plumbing parts from her local home-improvement store, the designer assembled two striking and very sturdy candlesticks.

DESIGNER:
SHEILA ENNIS

WHAT YOU NEED

2 lead plumbing pipes, ¾ inch (1.9 cm) wide and 5 to 6 inches (12.5 to 15 cm) long

2 lead flanges

2 large lead couplings

2 lead fittings

2 flat and pegged candles

WHAT YOU DO

1
To assemble each candlestick, screw the pipe into the flange to create the base.

2
Slide the coupling onto the pipe so it rests on the base.

3
Screw the fitting to the top to give the piece more definition.

"Tomorrow, and tomorrow, and tomorrow,
Creeps in this petty pace from day to day,
To the last syllable of recorded time
And all our yesterdays have lighted fools
The way to dusty death. Out, out brief candle!"

—WILLIAM SHAKESPEARE, *Macbeth*

WIRED-UP CANDLEHOLDERS

These spirited wire candleholders are easy to make and require a minimum of materials. Best of all, a simple twist of the pliers can take your works of art from silly to sophisticated. So go ahead—express yourself!

DESIGNER:
MAGGIE JONES

WHAT YOU NEED

14-gauge galvanized all-purpose wire

12-inch (30 cm) tapered candle

18-gauge steel wire

4 glass votive holders

4 votive candles

Wire cutters

Needle-nose pliers

WHAT YOU DO

FREESTANDING WIRE CANDLEHOLDER

1

Cut a 4-foot (1.2 m) piece of 14-gauge wire.

2

Using the pliers, bend a curlicue and wrap the wire around the bottom 2 inches (5 cm) of the candle.

3

Remove the candle and create a half flower-petal design on one side of the center.

4

Bring the wire to the center and create a symmetrical form on the opposite side.

5

Curve the last stretch of the wire around a petal and back toward the center, and intertwine it with the first 2-inch (5 cm) tall spiral. Make small curlicues at each end of the wire to tuck in any sharp points.

6

Cut about 2 feet (60 cm) of 18-gauge wire. Make a curlicue in the end of the wire, and then wrap it around the candle from top to base. End the wrap with a curlicue.

7

Wedge the wire-wrapped candle into the base of the candleholder, and bend the wire base until the candle stands upright and steady.

HANGING VOTIVES

8

Cut another piece of 14-gauge wire at least 4 feet (1.2 m) long. This will be the wire you will wrap around the votive holders.

9

Starting from the center of the length of wire, bend the wire down symmetrically on each side, then bend this center piece backwards and around on itself to form a nearly closed loop. The second piece of wire used for hanging will go through this loop. TIP: Bend the wire smoothly and don't allow the wire to become bent at a sharp angle—it's very difficult to straighten out.

10

Holding a votive holder on one side, bend one loose end of the wire down and around the glass cup once or twice. This will hold the votive cup in place.

11

After making at least one full revolution around the glass votive holder, begin to bend the wire up to the other side of the votive in an eye-pleasing design. Bring the wire back up to the height of the center top bend where you started, and curve the ends down and around to make another loop for the hanging wire to pass through.

12

Repeat the process on the other side.

13

To fashion the hanging hoop, cut an 18-inch (45 cm) piece of 14-gauge wire, and bend it into a circle without attaching the ends. Next, pull one end of the circle through the three looped bends of the votive wire. Then, take the ends of the circle and form intertwined curlicues to close the circle.

VOTIVES

14

Cut a piece of 14-gauge wire, about 12 inches (30 cm) long. Make a curlique in one end of the wire, and then wrap the rest of the wire around the glass holder. Repeat to make a second votive wrap.

Tips to Limit Wax Drips

Of course, buying dripless candles is the best way to avoid wax drips. However, sometimes an eye-catching candle just happens to be of the drip variety (chunk candles are notorious for their drippy nature). At other times our creative muse calls out for dripped candle wax as a fascinating way to decorate bottles or other surfaces. Here are a few tips to keep unintended drips to a minimum.

❯ *Change candles before they burn too low.*

❯ *Extinguish flames by snuffing rather than blowing, and you'll be less likely to get wax on surrounding linens and furniture.*

❯ *Use a bobèche, a decorative "collar" of metal or glass that slips over your candle, preventing wax from dripping on your candleholder.*

Right: Pamela Brown found dozens of these copper objects (anyone know what they are?) at a metal salvage yard. With the addition of a pegged candle, the discarded metal part became a gorgeous candleholder.

GARDEN TORCHES

These handsome garden lights are perfect for accenting a garden or lining an outdoor path.

DESIGNER
PAMELA BROWN

WHAT YOU NEED

(for one torch)

Black aluminum screening, approx. 13 x 17 inches (32.5 x 42.5 cm)

½-inch (1.3 cm) diameter copper piping, 5 feet (1.5 m)

⅝-inch (1.6 cm) hose clamp

18-gauge copper wire, 4 to 6 feet (1.2 to 1.8 m)

½-inch (1.3 cm) floor flange

½-inch (1.3 cm) male adapter

Metal washers (optional)

Thin-gauge wire (optional)

Pillar candle, 2 inches (5 cm) wide

Small container candle (optional; see page 50)

Scissors or wire cutters

Stapler (optional)

Hot-glue gun (optional)

WHAT YOU DO

1

Wrap the aluminum screen into a cone shape with an opening at the narrow end large enough to fit over the end of the copper pipe.

2

Place the screen cone over the end of the copper pipe so that about 6 inches (15 cm) of the pipe is inside the cone. Tighten the hose clamp around the bottom of the cone so that it will remain secure on the pipe.

3

Wrap copper wire tightly and evenly above the clamp up to 3 to 4 inches (7.5 to 10 cm) from the top of the pipe. Make sure the cone is open enough to accommodate the floor flange (see step 6). Cut the wire with scissors or wire cutters, and secure the end under the wrapped wire. Remove the hose clamp.

4

Crimp the top edges of the screen by folding them over by hand and pressing them in place.

5

Secure the overlapping ends of the screen by either threading the screen with a piece of copper wire or securing with a stapler.

6

Place a male adapter on the end of the copper pipe (inside the screen cone); then connect the floor flange to the male adapter. The floor flange will create a flat surface on which the candle will sit. The detail photo provides a close-up view of the torch construction.

7

To provide additional embellishment, you can tie on some metal washers, using the fine-gauge wire.

8

Once the torch is securely positioned in the ground (and level), place a pillar candle or a container candle on the floor flange (see page 50 for instructions on making container candles). TIP: You can use citronella oil in these candles to help discourage flying insects.

9

If you want, you can place a small amount of hot glue on the bottom of the container candle to hold it in place.

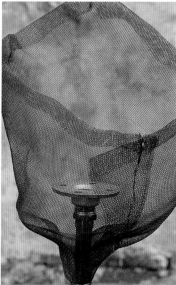

CONTAINER CANDLES

VICTORIAN JEWELED TEACUP CANDLE

Think you're too old for tea parties? Take a look at this enchanting teacup candle and think again! Along with the fun of decorating with costume jewelry, you'll get the satisfaction of pouring your own candle to fill this one-of-a-kind candleholder.

DESIGNER
ANNE McCLOSKEY

WHAT YOU NEED

Paraffin wax*

Brown crayons, paper wrapper removed

Saucepan or small pot

Stirring utensil

Oven mitts or pot holders

Teacup (old or new) with matching saucer

Costume jewelry (pearl strands, rhinestone earrings, etc.)

Wick tab

Wire-core wick, at least 4 inches (10 cm) long*

Cyanoacrylate glue

Wire cutters

*Refer to page 50 for more detailed instructions about making container candles. Be sure to test your teacup in advance to make sure it can withstand the heat of the melted wax.

WHAT YOU DO

1
In a pot over low heat, melt a chunk of paraffin wax—enough to fill the teacup halfway.

2
Break the brown crayons into small pieces and add them to the wax. Stir the wax until it becomes brown.

3
Position the wick in the cup as described on page 52.

4
Using the oven mitts to grab the pot, carefully pour the hot wax into the teacup, filling it about halfway. Gently shake the teacup to level the wax. When the wax has congealed and set, cut the wick down.

5
With the wire cutters, remove any backings on your jewelry pieces so that they will lie flat when glued. Cut up necklaces and earrings to form individual pieces and strands.

6
Apply glue to several jewelry bits at a time, letting the glue sit a moment to become very tacky. Press the pieces onto the outside of the teacup until you're pleased with the arrangement. TIP: Make sure that the jewelry is arranged in such a way that the cup will still be able to sit flat on the saucer.

7
Apply a generous dab of glue to the bottom of the teacup and hold it firmly in place on the saucer while it sets. Cluster pearl strands and remaining bits of jewelry around the edge of the saucer, and glue them in place.

Making Container Candles

Knowing how to make a container candle opens up many easy and creative ways to make a candleholder simply by pouring hot wax into a favorite container. The choices are nearly limitless when it comes to choosing the size and style of your container—from an antique perfume bottle to a favorite seashell.

There are a few things to take into consideration when choosing a container. In order for it to accommodate a candle, the container's opening must not be too small (anything smaller than 2 inches [5 cm] in diameter is too hard to light); the material from which it's made must be able to withstand the pouring temperature of the wax and be nonflammable; and the container must be able to stop the flow of wax.

Far right, Oriental food cans make great containers for candles. Many ethnic foods come in colorful and attractive cans. Use the food to prepare a tasty meal, and enjoy candlelight that complements your culinary adventure.

Choosing a Wick and Wick Tab

After you've chosen a container, you'll need the appropri-ate wick tabs and wire-core wicks to fit the size of the container. Wick tabs hold the wick to the bottom of the container while the wax is poured and help keep the wick upright. Wire-core wick is a special type of wick that has a stiff wire at its center. The wire allows the wick to stand upright, so it doesn't fall over and extinguish itself while burning.

Wick tabs are available in several sizes, and should be chosen according to the size of your wick. Your wick, in turn, should be chosen according to the size of your container; it's important to use the right size wick in order for the candle to burn correctly. Use small wire-core wicks for containers that are about 3 inches (7.5 cm) in diameter, medium wire-core wicks for containers 4 to 5 inches (10 to 12.5 cm) in diameter, and large wire-core wick for containers 6 inches (15 cm) in diameter. For containers larger than 6 inches (15 cm) in diameter, use two or more medium wire-core wicks.

Selecting the Wax

The key to a good container candle lies in the wax used to make it. While complex wax combinations and formulas exist for making candles, here's a good general rule of thumb to follow: A paraffin wax with a low melting point is best for container candles. The ideal melting point for the wax is 128°F (53°C).

Making the Candle

Now that you've got your container, your wick, and your wax, put them all together, and—voila! You've made a container candle all your own.

WHAT YOU NEED

Container of your choice to hold the candle

Paraffin wax, approximately ½ pound (228 g); amount will vary, depending on the size of your container

Double-boiler setup

Knife

Candy thermometer

Candle dye (optional)

Scented oil (optional)

Mold sealer (optional)

Wick tab

Wire-core wick

Straightened length of wire coat hanger

Rubber gloves

Ladle or metal cup with a handle

Thin nail

Scissors

Stove

WHAT YOU DO

1

The first step in making any container candle is to make sure the container will stand up to hot wax. The best way to do this is to fill the container with near-boiling water; if it holds up to this temperature, it will make a great candleholder.

Melting the Wax

2

To melt the wax, heat water over medium heat in the bottom of a double-boiler setup on the stove. Chop the wax into pieces with a knife. Place the wax pieces in the top of the doubleboiler.

3

Clip the candy thermometer

to the side of the pan, and heat the wax until it reaches 160° to 180°F (71° to 82°C). Do not leave the pot unattended for any reason while the hot wax is melting! It's very important that the wax not get too hot. The flash point, the point at which wax will ignite, varies for different types of wax; make sure you know the flash point for your wax before you begin.

4

If you're coloring the candle, melt the dye separately, then add it to the melted wax. Add any scented oils to the wax at this point, if desired.

Preparing the Wick and Tab

5

If your container has a hole in the bottom, such as a terra-cotta pot, fill it in with mold sealer, a pliable putty made specifically for sealing wick holes in molds and containers. Cut a piece of wick to fit the container, with a little extra to wrap around the coat-hanger wire. When the wax is completely melted and has reached the correct temperature, prime the wick by dipping it into the wax. When the wick has cooled, secure one end to a wick tab.

Pouring the Wax

6

Turn off the heat on the stove. Put a rubber glove on the hand that will be holding the container to insulate it from the heat of the melted wax. Warm the outside of the container by holding it under warm tap water for a few moments to prepare it for the temperature of the melted wax.

7

Pick up the container in one hand, and pour a small amount of melted wax into the bottom of the container. Use the coat-hanger to press the wick tab firmly into the wax. Pour in a little more wax to completely cover the wick tab. Position the coat-hanger wire across the top of the container, and wrap the other end of the wick around it to keep the wick centered.

8

Using a cup or ladle, pour the wax into the container until it's filled to the desired point.

9

As the candle cools, a small well will form in the center of the candle. Check the candle every few minutes. When the well forms, pierce the wax around the wick with a thin nail, being sure to pierce the wax all the way to the bottom of the container. Bring the wax back up to pouring temperature and fill the well with melted wax. Repeat this process until a well no longer forms.

10

Allow the candle to cool completely, then trim the wick to ½ or ¼ inch (1.3 or .6 cm).

Lark publisher Carol Taylor dreamed of a collection of kitchen items filled with candle wax, so we cooked up an assortment of container candles to make her dream come true.

TERRA-COTTA CANDLE POTS

These elegant container candles are easy to make and look wonderful in the garden or around the dinner table—the more the merrier.

DESIGNER
SHEILA ENNIS

WHAT YOU NEED

Terra-cotta pots and saucers, clean and dry

Small soft-bristle paintbrush

Old paintbrush

220-grit sandpaper

Materials for making container candles (see page 50)

FOR RED WITH SILVER LEAF POTS:

Burgundy acrylic spray paint

Silver or aluminum leaf*

Raw umber acrylic paint

Acrylic medium or glazing liquid*

*sold in art-supply stores and most craft-supply stores

FOR CRACKLE POTS:

Crackle medium*

Light green (celadon) latex semi-gloss paint

Raw umber acrylic paint

Acrylic medium or glazing liquid*

*sold in art-supply stores and most craft-supply stores

WHAT YOU DO

RED WITH SILVER LEAF POTS

1

Spray the entire pot, inside and out, and the saucer (if you're using one) with burgundy paint, and let dry thoroughly.

2

Apply the silver or aluminum leaf, following the directions on the package. Use any brush to apply the adhesive, but use a clean, soft one for the silver leaf. Use a soft touch, too. Don't put any leaf on the lip or inside of the pot. TIP: Don't completely cover the area with silver leaf; leaving some blank spots lets the undercoat color come through.

3

Sand the pot very lightly—just to knock the shine off the leaf. You want to create the effect of old silver, not stainless steel.

4

Make a translucent glaze mixture by diluting a small amount of raw umber with the clear medium. Don't put much color in the glaze; you want a very light tint. Too much color gives the pot a dull look. Apply the raw umber glaze, and let dry.

CRACKLE POTS

5

Apply the crackle medium to the outside of the pot and the saucer; let it set until the medium is tacky to the touch.

6

Apply the green paint. Try to be uniform in your brush strokes. The paint will crackle, revealing the terra-cotta finish underneath. Let dry.

7

Sand out any patchy areas. Sand all the edges to give the pot an aged look.

8

Apply the raw umber glaze, if you desire; here again you want just a lightly tinted glaze. Let the glaze dry.

Making the Candles

9

Follow the instructions on page 50.

GLASS

Everyone seems to wind up with a collection of inexpensive glass vases—all that remains of flowers we received on birthdays and anniversaries. Put them to good use as candleholders, and let them remind you of those special celebrations.

HERB-FILLED CANDLEHOLDER

Give someone special a two-in-one gift with this attractive and aromatic candleholder. Inside are layers of herbs, and on top is a lovely candle.

DESIGNER
SUSAN KINNEY

WHAT YOU NEED

Nicely shaped glass bottle*

Assorted herbs and seasonings, such as thyme, cracked red pepper, and minced garlic

1 piece of raffia, about 15 inches (37.5 cm) long

Taper candle

*Choose one with an opening large enough to fit a standard taper.

WHAT YOU DO

1

Pour the herbs and seasonings into the bottle, one variety at a time. Pour each herb to a thickness of about 1 inch (2.5 cm).

2

Tie the raffia around the bottle.

3

Insert the candle.

BEADED-FRINGE VOTIVE HOLDER

Creating a colorful fringe of beads is easy to do and can turn a plain wire frame into a carnival-looking candleholder.

DESIGNER
ALLISON STILWELL

WHAT YOU NEED

Glass votive with metal frame

100 to 200 assorted, small glass beads and charms

Beading needle

Cyanoacrylate glue

Scissors

Votive candle

WHAT YOU DO

1

Tie one end of the beading thread with a tight knot to the top of the metal frame. Thread a beading needle through the other end of the thread.

2

String an arrangement of beads onto this thread to a length you desire.

3

Add the charms or larger beads to the end of the string. Now insert the needle back up through the beads that you just strung. Take the thread over the top of the frame, back through the top bead, and back over the top of the frame.

4

Repeat this procedure to make another string of beads. Continue stringing beads until there is a fringe of beads all the way around the frame.

5

When the thread starts to get short, tie it to the frame with a knot, and thread the end down a string of beads. Add a drop of glue to the knot. Then, knot on a new piece of string and start again.

" 'Yes, I answered you last night;
'No,' this morning, sir, I say
Colors seen by candlelight
Will not look the same by day."
— ELIZABETH BARRETT BROWNING (1806–1861)
"The Lady's 'Yes' "

CELESTIAL VOTIVES

Create your own constellations with a simple painting technique on glass. When the candles in the votives are lit, this trio shines like a star-filled sky.

DESIGNER
DIANA LIGHT

WHAT YOU NEED

Glass votives

Black acrylic enamel*

Fine-pointed paintbrush

Scrap of paper

Votive candles

*The designer prefers Liquitex Glossies Acrylic Enamels

WHAT YOU DO

1
Practice painting shapes on a scrap of paper before you start to paint.

2
Using the photograph as a guide or a design of your own, paint stars, shooting stars, and other celestial images on the glass votives. Let dry.

3
Follow the instructions on the bottle for baking the votives in the oven to cure the paint.

STAINED GLASS WINDOW VOTIVE

Still can't persuade the Notre Dame Cathedral to sell you the Rose Window? Well, you won't need it once you light a votive inside this beautiful candleholder. Candlelight shimmers through the glass marbles, imitating the effect of a stained glass window.

DESIGNER
CATHY SMITH

WHAT YOU NEED

½-inch (1.3 cm) clear colored marbles: 116 dark blue, 108 turquoise, 58 yellow, and 26 red

Poster board

Masking tape

Silicone adhesive, non-flammable, clear-drying, in applicator tube

Toothpicks

Shoe box

Square glass ashtray, about 5 x 5 inches (12.5 x 12.5 cm)

Ruler

Scissors

Glass votive candleholder

Votive candle

WHAT YOU DO

1
Assemble poster board forms for the side panels. Cut a 5½ x

9 inch (13.8 x 22.5 cm) rectangle for the large panel and a 5 x 9 inch (12.5 x 22.5 cm) rectangle for the small panel. Fold and crease each side of the rectangle ½ inch (1.3 cm) in from the edge of the panel. Make a horizontal cut along the edge of the folded border on each of the four corners. Fold the forms up at the edges, and tape the flaps to form two boxes. One box should measure 4 x 8 x ½ inch (10 x 20 x 1.3 cm) and the other should measure 4½ x 8 x ½ inch (11.3 x 20 x 1.3 cm).

Figure 1

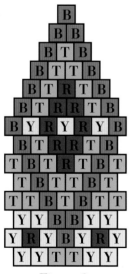

Figure 2

2

Lay out the marbles in the pattern provided (see figures 1 and 2) or create your own. It helps to have the form tilted slightly downward to keep the marbles from rolling around. (Propping a thick paperback book under the panel works well.) Each row of marbles rests "between" the previous row, meaning each marble in an upper row will rest in the space formed by the joining of two marbles beneath it.

3

Glue the marbles together using a neat, thin bead of silicone adhesive. While gluing, use a six-ray star pattern to make sure each marble is securely glued to its neighbors. A line of glue should connect the marble to each of its top two neighbors, each of its side neighbors, and each of its bottom two neighbors.

4

Allow the glue to cure for 12 hours. Gently remove the sides from the forms. You will notice that the sides are quite floppy. Flip them over to the front side (the side with no adhesive). Use a toothpick to neatly dab a very small amount of glue between each marble, following the same star ray pattern used on the back; this reinforces the bond and keeps the panels from being so flexible. The less glue used at this stage, the better.

5

Assemble the panels. Use any right-angle item, such as the shoe box, as a base for this step. Lay one marble panel flat, and stand the other panel up at a right angle to the first so that the staggered marble edges meet as closely as possible. Run a neat, continuous bead of glue along the inner corner where the staggered edges of the two panels meet. Be sure to achieve a secure bond. Repeat this procedure for the remaining two panels. Allow the silicone to cure for 12 hours before continuing.

6

Stand the panels on their bottom surface and join the other two corners together. Butt one unglued corner up against the inner corner of the shoe box for a base, and run a continuous bead of glue along the inside. Allow the glue to cure for 12 hours.

7

Turn the ashtray upside down and center the marble assembly on the bottom of the ashtray (which is now facing upward). Run a continuous bead of glue along the bottom inside edge of the marble assembly where it meets the glass ashtray. Glue the bottom of a votive candleholder to the upward-facing surface of the ashtray. Allow the glue to cure for 12 hours.

Iemanjá Festival

While revelers in Manhattan's Time Square brave the cold awaiting the descent of a gigantic apple to signal the start of a new year, thousands of Brazilians usher in the new 365-day cycle by paying tribute to a sea goddess on the country's moonlit beaches.

The followers of Umbanda, a religion practiced in Brazil, don white clothing for their seaside ceremonies, which begin at around 10 o'clock in the evening. Carrying fresh flowers, candles, and cachaça (sugarcane alcohol), they make their way down to the beaches, where they spread out tablecloths on the sand, cover them with gifts for the goddess, Iemanjá, and surround them with lit candles.

The ceremony peaks at midnight, when the worshippers rush into the sea, throwing the gifts and flowers into the waves, an act accompanied by a cacophony of sobbing, shrieking, and singing. If the offerings are carried out to sea by the waves, the followers return home happy, knowing that the goddess has been satisfied. The people interpret any flowers and gifts cast back upon the shore as an ill omen, however, and wonder uneasily what events the coming year will hold.

Photos courtesy of The Brazilian Embassy

ICE CREAM CANDLEHOLDER

As tempting as a scoop of vanilla ice cream, this pretty container candle is simple to create and can be repeated dozens of times using different types of glasses and beads.

DESIGNER
SUSAN KINNEY

WHAT YOU NEED

Assortment of glass and silver beads

Assortment of seed beads

3 or 4 earring findings*

26-gauge silver, gold, or copper jewelry wire

Attractive, sturdy wine glass or goblet

Wick

Wick tab

White bead wax**

Teaspoon

Round- or chain-nose pliers

Wire cutters or sharp scissors

*sold in bead-supply stores

**Bead wax is candle wax that has been granulated into small beads. It comes in a variety of colors and scents, and is sold in most craft- and candlemaking-supply stores.

WHAT YOU DO

1

Arrange your beads into three or four groupings that you like. Slip each grouping onto an earring finding. Use the pliers to make a small loop at the other end to hold the beads on the finding.

2

Wrap the jewelry wire around the neck of the wine glass three or four times. Slip one of the bead strands onto the wire and position it against the stem. Wrap the wire around the stem again; then slip on another bead strand. Continue in this manner until you have strung on all your bead strands.

3

Cut the wire to a length that will allow you to weave the end through the wrapped wire to tie it off.

4

Place the wick and wick tab into the bottom of the glass, making sure it is centered (see page 51 for more information about wicks).

5

Spoon the bead wax into the glass until it's nearly full.

6

Trim the wick so that only ½ inch (1.3 cm) remains above the wax beads.

Designer Maureen Donahue had the clever idea of turning two crackled glass tumblers upside down and filling them with glittery tinsel to create a pair of candlesticks. Round molded candles, coated with a special metallic paint, look especially glamorous perched on top.

AUTUMN LEAVES HURRICANE SHADE

Transforming an ordinary glass hurricane shade into an extraordinary candleholder is easier than you think. While this pattern is perfect for fall, you could create a summer look with sunflower stamps and bright colors, or pine trees and holiday hues for winter appeal.

DESIGNER
LYNN B. KRUCKE

WHAT YOU NEED

Polymer clay: translucent, olive green, and terra cotta

Glass hurricane shade

Autumn leaf stamp

Powdered pigment in metallic gold

Clear gloss latex spray enamel

Clear glass votive holder

Votive candle

Pasta machine or rolling pin

WHAT YOU DO

1

Condition the clay in the following amounts: $\frac{1}{2}$ block of translucent clay and $\frac{1}{16}$ block each of green and terra cotta. Knead each color separately until it's pliable.

2

Roll each color to form a snake. Place all three snakes side by side and roll them together. Then twist the three-stranded snake and roll it through the pasta machine on the thickest setting, or use the rolling pin to flatten the clay. Fold the resulting sheet in half and repeat until you are happy with the way it looks.

TIP: The translucent clay will allow light to come through your hurricane shade once it's baked. It's important not to over mix, as you will end up with one muddy color instead of streaks and contrasting lighter areas.

3

When you're happy with your mixture, roll it through the pasta machine on progressively higher settings up to #7, or continue to roll it with the rolling pin until the clay is as thin as possible without tearing. Your sheet will be very thin now, so handle it gently. If along the way it becomes too hard to handle, cut it in half and proceed with each piece separately.

4

Tear off small pieces of the clay sheet and place them over your hurricane shade to completely cover the outside. Press the edges together as you go to blend the seams.

5

Once the shade is completely covered with clay, randomly stamp leaves all over it using the leaf stamp. You will see visible impressions in the clay. Don't worry if each stamp doesn't transfer perfectly.

6

Next, roll one snake of green and one of terra cotta. Twist these together and wrap the rope around the top outer edge of the shade. Use leftover marbled clay to make a twisted rope to wrap around the bottom edge. Blend the seams where they join on the piece.

7

Bake as directed by the manufacturer of your clay. Allow it to cool completely.

8

With your finger, rub the metallic gold powder over the cooled piece; this will highlight the leaf impressions.

9

Spray the finished piece with the clear gloss latex spray enamel to seal it.

10

Place the hurricane shade over a clear glass votive holding a votive candle.

*A glass frog,
designed to hold
flowers, makes a
lovely candleholder.
Designer Susan
Kieffer suggests
using dripless can-
dles with this one.*

69

Celebrate the summer solstice (or any summer night) by setting your fireplace ablaze with dozens of candles.

70

ETCHED HOLLY BOWL

It's easy to create the look of etched glass, thanks to the new products on the market. This charming holiday bowl is perfect for floating candles or holding your favorite eggnog—just don't combine the two at the same time!

DESIGNER
LYNN B. KRUCKE

WHAT YOU NEED

Glass bowl

Adhesive shelf paper

Paper punch, holly design

Soft lint-free cloth

1-inch (2.5 cm) foam brush

Glass-etching cream

Ribbon

Floating candles

Hot-glue gun and glue sticks

WHAT YOU DO

1

Thoroughly wash and dry the glass bowl. The etching cream works best on very clean surfaces that are free of dirt and oils.

2

Punch the desired number of shapes out of the adhesive paper.

3

Remove the backing from the cut-outs to expose the adhesive, and position the shapes on the bowl. Use the lint-free cloth to press the images onto the glass.
TIP: The paper's crisp edges require that the shapes be completely adhered to the bowl.

4

Use the foam brush to cover the bowl with a thick layer of etching cream. Allow the bowl to sit for 25 to 30 minutes, then rinse off the cream. Peel off the shapes.

5

Dry the bowl. The etched part will be more obvious once the bowl has dried.

6

Fashion a full bow and hot glue it to the base of the bowl.

7

Fill the bowl with water and float your candles!

"As a white candle
In a holy place,
So is the beauty
Of an aged face."
—JOSEPH CAMPBELL
(1881-1944) *The Old Woman*

Advent

The twinkling of candlelight grows stronger week by week during the Christian holiday of Advent, a four-week period of preparation and meditation leading up to Christmas on December 25. Stemming from the Latin word, adventus, which means the coming or the arrival, the Advent rituals symbolize hope for the return of Christ.

As a display of their faith and as a marker of the approaching Christmas celebration, many families light the four candles of the Advent wreath. Made of woven evergreen boughs, the Advent wreath was traditionally hung by red ribbons from the ceiling, suspended parallel to the floor with the four candles standing upright. One candle is lit on the first Sunday closest to November 30; two of the candles on the following Sunday; three on the third Sunday; and all four candles burn on the final Sunday preceding Christmas Day.

Designer Perri Crutcher arranged this lovely non-traditional advent wreath, using a colorful assortment of fresh and dried flowers.

Like many Christian traditions, Advent customs have their roots in the Pagan rituals practiced by the inhabitants of eastern Europe in pre-Christian times. These Germanic tribes gathered evergreen wreaths during the cold winter darkness, and lit bonfires as signs of hope for the coming spring and the renewal of light to the earth. Christians carried on these folk practices, translating the hope for daylight into hope for the everlasting light of Christ.

The conventional Advent wreath holds three violet candles and one rose candle, but the use of four white candles or four violet candles is also popular today. The rose candle is usually lit on the third Sunday of Advent. As the candles are lit, a prayer may be said.

WOODEN MENORAH

Celebrate the joyful spirit of Hanukkah with this whimsical menorah. Or, add more or less holders and you can use this colorful candelabra all year round for any occasion.

DESIGNER
MAX KELLER

WHAT YOU NEED

Assorted wooden beads, candle cups, spools, and wheels*

Several colors of acrylic craft paint

Paintbrushes

Complementary shades of dimensional paint

Paper plates

Chenille stems

9 metal washers

Wood glue

Cotton swabs

1 precut wooden base*

Thin tapers or birthday candles

*available at craft-supply stores

WHAT YOU DO

1

Paint the wooden parts in various colors of craft paint, and let dry.

2

Decorate each piece with dimensional paint, using any of the color combinations and shapes approved by preschoolers all over the world! Set the pieces aside to dry. TIP: Squeeze a little paint from each bottle onto a paper plate before each application to reduce the pressure in them so that the paint will flow evenly.

3

Now play! Arrange the pieces in a way you like until you have created nine stacks of wooden pieces. While you experiment with the different possible combinations, it's helpful to thread a chenille stem through each stack to provide stability to your creations. Be sure to top each stack with a wooden piece that has a hole wide enough to fit a thin taper or birthday candle; place a washer under this piece.

4

Glue the pieces in each stack together with wood glue. Cotton swabs are handy for applying glue to smaller parts.

5

Paint the wooden base in a color that will complement the assorted holders. Let dry.

6

Glue the candleholders to the wooden base.

Kwanzaa

A candleholder known as a Kinara bears special significance for celebrants of Kwanzaa, an African-American spiritual holiday, held each year from

December 26 to January 1. Created by California State University professor Maulana Karenga in 1966, Kwanzaa offers people of African descent a way to honor and reconnect with their roots.

With spaces for seven candles, the Kinara symbolizes the continent of Africa, the place of origin for African-Americans. The seven candles used in the Kinara are known as the mishumaa saba, and reflect the traditional colors of Africa—one black, three red, and three green.

During the week-long holiday, family members gather in their homes each evening to discuss the principle of the day, one of the seven Nguzo Saba central to Kwanzaa: umoja (unity); kujichagulia (self-determination); ujima (collective work and responsibility); ujamaa (cooperative economics); nia (purpose); kuumba (creativity); and imani (faith). They then light one candle to symbolize giving light and life to each of the principles.

In addition to the Kinara, Kwanzaa celebrants may display the bendera, a tablecloth based on the African national flag. A straw mat known as the mkeka, a reminder of African traditions and history, serves as a space for other special symbols, such as the unity cup, or kikombi cha umoja. Ears of corn, called muhundi or vibunzi, reflect the number of children in the household, and green plants stand for the oneness between Africans and nature.

The Kwanzaa celebration culminates with a terrific feast of African or African-inspired foods known as Karamu, held on December 31. Bowls of fruit and vegetables crown table centerpieces, a reminder of the meaning of the Swahili word, Kwanzaa, "first fruits of the harvest." Traditional gift giving follows on January 1, when family members exchange enriching presents, such as African historical and cultural books or homemade heritage symbols. Such presents are called zawadi, and symbolize the key role of education and culture in Kwanzaa.

Hanukkah: The Jewish Festival of Lights

The eight-day celebration of Hanukkah, celebrated by Jews in mid-December, was born out of a specific, historically recorded, Greek-Jewish conflict. Israel had agreed to be ruled by Alexander the Great, rather than be brutally conquered. Jews embraced the Greek ideals of beauty, logic, and learning, and the Jews of that time became Hellenized. The only exception was the Jewish religion, which remained generally intact, because the Greeks didn't care about a conquered nation's religious practices.

In 168 BCE, something changed. The Greek/Syrian king decided that Greek gods would be substituted for the Jewish God. A Greek idol was erected in the Holy Temple of Jerusalem, and Jews were compelled to bring sacrifices to it. In and around Jerusalem, the Jewish population had become so assimilated, that many city dwellers didn't object.

But one family in the country openly revolted against the king. When the Greeks sent soldiers to quell this bothersome rebellion, they found themselves fighting citizen guerrillas. After several skirmishes, the Greek soldiers were beaten back by this small band of Jewish fighters, who came to be known as the Maccabees. Their message spread throughout the countryside. They re-instituted ritual prayer and demanded that Jews not only live their Judaism, but fight for it.

The rebellion grew until it arrived at the gates of Jerusalem. The Jews of the city joined the ranks of the Maccabees. Starting as a small group of about 600, they now stood against the Greeks as an army of 16,000! The Greeks were defeated, and began retreating to Syria for reinforcements. But the Maccabees pursued them and killed their king. The king's son admitted defeat, and took his army home. The Jews recaptured the Holy Temple and freed Jerusalem.

Because of the battles, the Jews had missed the important harvest festival of Succot. So Succot was held while they repaired and re-sanctified the Temple. That first Hanukkah—meaning rededication—was a great victory celebration, and included a late, eight-day Succot harvest festival. The Hanukkah menorah features nine places for candles; the ninth candle, called the shamesh, is used to light the other candles, one for each night of this important festival of light.

OH HANUKKAH

Oh Hanukkah, Oh Hanukkah

Come light the menorah

Let's have a party, well all dance the Horah

Gather 'round the table, we'll give you a treat

Sivivon to play with and latkes to eat

And while we are playing the candles are burning low

One for each night they shed a sweet light to remind us of days long ago.

77

KWANZAA KINARA

Painted in the bold, traditional colors of Africa, this attractive candle-holder makes a fine Kinara during the season of Kwanzaa, or a sturdy and handsome centerpiece any time of the year.

DESIGNERS
ROBIN CLARK AND CATHY SMITH

WHAT YOU NEED

2 x 4, 16 inches (40 cm) long

7 wooden candle cups; 3 measuring $1\frac{1}{4}$ x $1\frac{1}{2}$ inches (3 x 3.8 cm) and 4 measuring 1 x $1\frac{1}{4}$ inches (2.5 x 3 cm)*

Sandpaper

#8 round paintbrush

#0 and #1 round paintbrushes

Acrylic wood-tone stain

Acrylic paints: black, rusty red, green, mustard yellow

Pencil

Acrylic gloss varnish

7 wood screws (or wood glue)

Table saw

Drill with $\frac{3}{4}$-inch (1.9 cm) bit

Router with $\frac{1}{4}$-inch (.6 cm) round-over bit (optional)

*available from craft-supply stores

WHAT YOU DO

1
Cut the 2 x 4 to a width of $2\frac{3}{4}$ inches (6.9 cm).

2
Round over all the edges of the 2 x 4, or sand them down with sandpaper. If necessary, sand the candle cups.

3
Stain the wood base and candle cups. Allow to dry.

4
Paint the sides only of the base with two coats of mustard yellow, allowing the paint to dry between coats.

5
Draw your design on the base. The one shown here consists of simple stripes, squares, and rectangles in alternating colors. You may copy this design or paint one of your own.

6
Paint in the design using the #0 and #1 brushes as needed. Be sure to change your rinse water between colors so you don't muddy the colors. TIP: The red and green colors are translucent and may need two coats for good coverage. Allow the paint to dry completely.

7
Apply two coats of gloss varnish to the base and candle cups. Allow the varnish to dry completely before handling the pieces.

8
Using the pencil, draw a center-line the length of the 2 x 4. Mark the center point of the line, then mark a point 2 inches (5 cm) in each direction from the center point. Make two additional marks $1\frac{3}{4}$ inches (4.4 cm) on either side of the first two marks. You should end up with seven marks altogether.

9

If you plan to use screws to attach your candle cups, drill holes ¾ inch (1.9 cm) wide and 1 inch (2.5 cm) deep at each mark.

10

Mount the candle cups on the marked points using screws through the base of each cup (the head of the screw will be visible inside the cup base), or apply wood glue on the bottom of each cup. This designer positioned the three larger cups in the middle, and the smaller cups on the outside of the arrangement.

11

Place the candles in the Kinara as shown in the photograph.

PINE TREE CANDELABRA

Much to the delight of holiday guests, this modest wooden tree trans-
forms into a tower of glowing boughs with a simple twist of its
branches and the addition of thin tapers.

DESIGNER
ROBIN CLARK

WHAT YOU NEED

1 piece of cedar, $7\frac{1}{4}$ inches (18.2 cm) square, 1 inch (2.5 cm) thick

1 piece of cedar, $6\frac{1}{2}$ x $8\frac{1}{2}$ x $\frac{3}{4}$ inches (16.3 x 21.3 x 1.9 cm)

1 dowel, 6 x $\frac{1}{4}$ inches (15 x .6 cm)

Pencil

Acrylic paint: bright green, white, and purple

Paintbrushes

Sandpaper

2 screws, $1\frac{1}{4}$ inches (3 cm) long

9 tapers, $\frac{1}{2}$ inch (1.3 cm) wide

Drill with $\frac{1}{8}$-, $\frac{1}{4}$-, and $\frac{1}{2}$-inch (.3, .6 and 1.3 cm) bits

Band saw (or scroll saw)

Router with $\frac{1}{4}$-inch (.6 cm) roundover bit (or sandpaper)

Screwdriver

WHAT YOU DO

1

Stand the square cedar block up on one edge. Drill a $\frac{1}{4}$-inch (.6 cm) wide, 6-inch-long (15 cm) centered hole in the middle of the edge at an equal distance from each end of the square.

2

Lay the square down flat and draw the tree pattern. It does not have to be perfectly symmetrical, but you should draw pieces that will be easy to cut out and will fit perfectly atop one another.

3

Using the band saw, cut out each piece of the tree. Round over the pieces with the router or sandpaper.

4

Drill $\frac{1}{2}$-inch (1.3 cm) holes, $\frac{1}{2}$ inch (1.3 cm) deep, in each outside edge of the tree limbs and at the very top of the top section (you will simply be widening the existing dowel hole.) You should wind up with nine of these holes.

5

Paint the individual pieces green, and let dry.

6

Arrange the pieces so that they fit atop one another. Insert the $\frac{1}{4}$-inch (.6 cm) wide, 6-inch (15 cm) long dowel into the $\frac{1}{2}$-inch (1.3 cm) hole running through the middle of the pieces. The dowel will hold the pieces together and let them pivot.

7

To make the base, saw the corners off the 6-$\frac{1}{2}$ x 8-$\frac{1}{2}$ x $\frac{3}{4}$ inch (16.3 x 21.3 x 1.9 cm) block of wood about $\frac{3}{8}$ inch (.9 cm) from the edge. Use the router or sandpaper to round over the edges.

8

Paint the base purple and let it dry.

9

Drill two $\frac{1}{8}$-inch (.3 cm) pilot holes, centered, $1\frac{3}{4}$ inches (4.4 cm) in from each narrow end. Line up the bottom section of the tree structure with the holes, and mark corresponding points on the bottom section. Drill two $\frac{1}{8}$-inch (.3 cm) holes at these points. Then, hold the tree assembly upside down, matching up the holes of the base and the bottom section, and secure with the screws. (Secure the screws from the bottom of the base.)

10

Add a light coat of white paint to the assembled structure, and let dry. Then lightly sand off some of the paint to give the tree its folk-art appearance.

PUNCHED COPPER JACK-O-LANTERN

Trick-or-treaters will know you're in the Halloween spirit when they discover this grinning jack-o-lantern on your front porch or in a window, its ghoulish glow casting a perfect holiday spell.

DESIGNER
CATHY SMITH

WHAT YOU NEED:

9 x 12-inch (22.5 x 30 cm) sheet of copper

Board or plywood, at least 10 x 13 inches (25 x 32.5 cm)

7-inch (17.5 cm) diameter round wood for base

Masking tape

Thumb tacks

Transfer paper (optional)

Fine-grade sandpaper

Automotive adhesive*

Paintbrushes

Black acrylic paint

Clear gloss acrylic varnish

¾-inch (1.9 cm) copper pipe cap**

#000 steel wool

6-inch (15 cm) tall candle

Awl or punch tool

Small hammer or rubber mallet

Straightedge or sturdy ruler

Tin snips

Needle-nose pliers, with jaws taped to avoid scratching copper

Drill with bit to rout channel in base, or a ¼-inch (.6cm) chisel or wood-carving tool

*available at home-improvement centers

**available at plumbing-supply stores

WHAT YOU DO

Punching the Copper Sheet

1

Tape the corners and edges of the copper sheet to protect your hands.

2

Fasten the copper to the board or plywood with tape or with thumbtacks placed in the wood around the edges of the copper sheet—not through the metal itself. Tape the pattern in place or trace it onto the copper using transfer paper.

Enlarge to 200%

83

3

Using the awl and hammer or the mallet, punch holes through the copper, following the pattern. You'll be punching through the front side of the copper. Try to keep the taps uniform so the holes will be the same size. Double check to be sure you've punched all the holes in the pattern.

4

Remove the tape or thumbtacks. Turn the copper plate over so that the back side is facing up. Using the awl and straightedge, heavily score lines in the copper ¼ inch (.6 cm) in from the side and top edges. With the tin snips, notch both of the top corners, and remove them. Cut the top edge only into a "fringe," making cuts at ⅛ inch (.3 cm) intervals all the way across. Use the taped needle-nose pliers to fold over the scored and fringed edges. (The fringe keeps the copper from buckling when curved, and folding keeps the sheet edges from being hazardous.) Crease the fold with the pliers.

5

Gently roll the copper sheet into a cylinder until it will hold a cylindrical shape on its own. Be careful about forming buckles and dents around heavily punched areas (these are easily pushed out by hand.)

Preparing the Base

6

Use a drill or chisel to carve a ¼-inch (.6 cm) deep channel on the wood base, 1 inch (2.5 cm) in from the outer circumference of wood. The channel will end up with a 5-inch (12.5 cm) diameter. You can leave about 3 inches (7.5 cm) uncarved, as the copper cylinder will be open in the back and won't require the full circle.

7

Sand the base. Fill the channel with adhesive, and insert the bottom edge of the copper sheet into the channel. Make sure that the structure is stable. Allow the glue to dry and cure; this may take several hours.

8

Cover the bottom of the copper shade with tape, and paint the base black. Allow the paint to dry. Finish the base with gloss varnish, and allow it to dry completely.

9

Glue the copper cap, cup-side up, to the center of the base.

10

Burnish the front of the copper shade with the steel wool to remove any fingerprints.

Rob Pulleyn's simple but elegant candleholders bring a touch of winter greenery inside the home. He painted the terra-cotta pots with white paint diluted with a little water, and let them dry. Then he glued the leaves and berries in place, and illuminated the pots with votive candles.

Cleaning Up Candle Wax Drips

*R*ecently, during a special dinner at my house, I heard a small, familiar, and ghastly sound...wax cascading down the caved-in side of a beeswax candle. A waterfall of hot wax poured onto the wall from the window ledge on which the candle was perched.

Fortunately, as part of the research for this book, I had just learned about several proven methods to remove candle wax from nearly any surface, including walls, wood floors, tiles, and your grandmother's hand-embroidered white table linens.

Most candle lovers would agree that the invention of dripless candles rates right up there with the discovery of a new planet. All other candles will drip if they're not labeled "dripless." Always wait until the wax has cooled and hardened completely before trying the methods described below.

REMOVING WAX FROM CARPET AND UPHOLSTERY

First, use a dull knife to scrape as much of the wax off as possible without damaging the carpet or fabric. Place a brown paper bag, absorbent paper towel, or napkin over the wax (do not use newspaper—the ink will color the carpet). Place a medium-warm iron on top of the paper and move it back and forth (fiber damage could occur if the iron is left in one place for too long). In a few moments, the wax will melt and transfer to the paper.

Depending on the size of the spot, you may want to keep changing the paper towels or bags as they become soiled with the melted wax. Next, sponge the spot with a small amount of dry-cleaning solvent, and blot with a dry cloth. Be sure to use small amounts of solvent to prevent any possible damage to sizings, backings, or stuffing materials. Do not use gasoline, lighter fluid, or carbon tetrachloride. Finally, mix one teaspoon of a neutral detergent (a mild detergent containing no alkalies or bleaches) with a cup of lukewarm water and blot the spot with this mixture.

REMOVING WAX FROM TABLE LINENS

This process is similar to removing wax from carpet and upholstery, except that in this case you have two sides to work with instead of one. Start by using a dull knife or plastic card to scrape off as much of the wax as possible. Then, place a brown paper bag, absorbent paper towel, or napkin under the wax stain, and another one over the stain. Press the stain with a warm iron, moving it back and forth slightly to avoid scorching. The iron will melt the wax into the paper. Replace the paper with new sheets as it becomes soaked with the melted wax. If a colored dye stain remains, mix one part denatured alcohol with two parts water, and sponge the stain with this mixture. If the item is washable, wash it in warm, sudsy water. If not, simply sponge it with a dry-cleaning solvent.

REMOVING WAX FROM HARDWOOD FLOORS AND WOOD FURNITURE

Trying to wipe up freshly dripped wax on wood will usually only leave you with a bigger stain. What you want to do is to harden the wax as quickly as possible before you try to remove it. The first step is to place some ice cubes in a plastic bag. Hold the bag against the dripped wax for a few seconds to freeze it; the wax should become brittle. Wipe up any water drips immediately. Then, use a dull knife, spoon, or plastic spatula to very gently scrape the wax off the wooden surface. Take care not to scratch the surface. A plastic credit card also works well for this purpose, but be sure to hold the card in both hands, tilt it slightly, and scrape very gen-

tly in order to avoid gouging the surface.

You may use mineral spirits or naphtha to remove any remaining wax. Buff this area of the floor after all the wax has been removed. To restore the wooden surface, saturate 000 steel wool with furniture wax and vigorously rub the stained area. Polish the area, following the grain of the wood, and wipe it dry with a clean cloth.

REMOVING WAX FROM WALLS

Follow the same procedure as for hardwood floors, but skip the steel wool and furniture wax.

REMOVING WAX FROM CERAMIC TILE

Bathrooms are a popular place for enjoying candles. If wax drips onto the tile, start by using a piece of soft wood, such as a craft stick, to scrape off as much dried wax as possible. Next, use a hand-held lighter to heat the wax and melt it. Once the wax has returned to a liquid state,

clean it up with a rag. The tile can't be damaged by the lighter, because the tile has been fired at a much higher temperature than the lighter's flame will ever reach.

REMOVING WAX FROM CANDLEHOLDERS

To many, this chore seems as ironic as it is difficult. However, restoring your candleholders to their original, non-wax-covered state need not be so daunting. To clean candle wax out of a votive cup, soak the cup in hot, soapy water for 30 to 45 minutes, then scrub with a cloth to remove the wax.

To clean dripped wax out of the curves and crevices of metal candlesticks, put the candleholders in the freezer. The wax can be peeled off easily once it freezes.

BOTTLES, POTS & CANS

SODA CAN CANDLEHOLDERS

Wondering what to do with all those aluminum cans overflowing in your recycling bin? Why, make more candleholders, of course! These gilded beauties are great for decorating a table for a party.

DESIGNER
MAGGIE JONES

WHAT YOU NEED

Aluminum soda cans, rinsed

Non-flammable gold spray paint

Votive candles

Small, sharp scissors

Large screwdriver

Hammer

WHAT YOU DO

1

Insert the scissors into the mouth opening of the soda can and cut to the edge of the top of the can. TIP: Be very careful while cutting the cans—aluminum edges are very sharp!

2

Cut around the flat surface of the top of the can, trying to retain as much of the can's height as possible.

3

Place the handle end of a large screwdriver in the bottom of the can while it's standing up. Hammer the tip of the screwdriver shaft in order to flatten the can's concave bottom so that a votive candle can sit steadily on the surface.

4

Cut down one side of the can in a curved or geometric cut to about 1 inch (2.5 cm) from the can's bottom.

5

Make a second cut about ¼ inch (.6 cm) away from the first cut in a parallel line or in a different shape. Continue cutting strips around the can until the entire can has been cut.

6

Bend the strips down and out, curling or twisting them as you like.

7

Spray the entire can, inside and out, with gold paint. Two coats may be necessary.

8

Place a votive candle in each of these cans.

TIP: Variations can be made by using different colors of paint or by hot-gluing beads or sequins to the can.

GARDEN PARTY LANTERN

Simple painting and drilling are all that are required to turn an ordinary watering can into a charming centerpiece candleholder, perfect for your next garden party.

DESIGNER
ANNE MCCLOSKEY

WHAT YOU NEED

Large metal watering can

Medium-grade sandpaper

Paper towels

Acrylic paints in yellow, yellow-orange, pink, purple, and lime green

Acrylic gloss varnish

Paintbrushes

Sponge brush

Permanent black marker

Pillar candle or votives

Electric drill with spiral-cut bit or $1/8$-inch (.3 cm) bit

Wood block to fit inside watering can

Center punch

WHAT YOU DO

1

Start with a clean and dry watering can. Sand the entire can with sandpaper, wiping off the loose particles with a damp paper towel.

2

Apply two coats of yellow paint to the body and handle. Let dry.

3

Paint your flower design. The design shown here is a mixture of freehand circles, petals, and dabbed sponge-brush blotches. When the paint is completely dry, apply two coats of acrylic gloss varnish.

4

Decide where you want to drill holes in the watering can and use the black marker to mark them. The best places for holes are around the flowers. The more holes you make, the more candlelight will shine through the can.

5

Use the center punch to mark the points to be drilled.

6

Place the block of wood inside the can while drilling; this prevents the can from caving in around where you are drilling. Use the drill and bit of your choice to drill holes at the marked points.

7

Place small votives or larger pillar candles in the watering can, or try a citronella candle to keep bugs away on warm summer evenings.

PAINTED BOTTLE WITH PETALS

This clever design for creating candlesticks gives those about-to-be recycled plastic bottles new purpose and appeal. With just a few supplies, you can turn soda pop into pop art!

DESIGNER
COLLEEN WEBSTER

WHAT YOU NEED

(for each candlestick)

20 fl oz (600 mL) clean and empty plastic soda bottle*

Scrap of ½-inch (1.3 cm) plywood, 4½ square (11.3 cm square)

Sandpaper

Sponge brush

Wood primer

Acrylic paint: black and bright gold

Flat paintbrush, ½ inch (1.3 cm) wide

Polyurethane

Taper or flat candle

Scissors

Staple gun with staples

*The designer used a Dr. Pepper® bottle to take advantage of the striped pattern.

WHAT YOU DO

1

Sand the wood base.

2

Use the sponge brush to prime the base. Let it dry.

3

Remove the cap ring from the bottle. Cut the bottle about 4 inches (10 cm) down from the top of the mouth. Save the bottom portion.

4

Cut 14 vertical slits in the bottle, ½ inch (1.3 cm) deep and 1 inch (2.5 cm) apart (see figure 1). You will now have 14 tabs; bend up each tab.

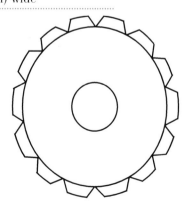

Figure 1

Figure 2

5

Take the bottom portion of the bottle and cut out six or seven petal shapes, using the natural curve at the bottom. Trim each petal so it's at least 2¾ (7 cm) long.

6

Place the bottle top on the wood base, and tuck one petal at a time underneath, with the curved part pointing up. To secure the bottle and petals to the base, staple through the tab and the flat part of the petal into the wood (see figure 2). Staple each petal evenly around the bottle, making sure the staples are flush with the wood base.

7

Paint the bottle, petals, and base black. Let dry.

8

Following the pattern on the bottle, paint the gold stripes. Let dry. If necessary, apply a second coat.

9

Paint the petals and the nozzle gold, and let dry. Paint the edges of the wood base gold, and let dry.

10

Apply one to two coats of polyurethane, and let dry.

TIN CAN FLOWERS

Light a candle in these recycled cans and your garden will bloom year-round! Fun and easy to make, these charming flower candleholders will add cheer to a winter table or brighten a garden path in summer.

DESIGNER
ANNE MCCLOSKEY

WHAT YOU NEED

3 tin cans, cleaned, with labels
    removed

Cotton utility gloves

Surface conditioner

Enamel craft paints:
    green, yellow, ocher,
    fuchsia, medium pink, and
    light pink

Small paintbrushes

Glass glaze

Cyanoacrylate glue

2 glass votive cups

2 votive candles

Strong shears for cutting metal*

Needle-nose pliers

*Note: Be careful when cutting metal; the edges can be sharp. Wearing gloves while cutting metal may offer some protection.

WHAT YOU DO

SUNFLOWER CANDLEHOLDER

Two cans are needed to create this design—one will be inserted into the other to create layers of petals.

1

Use the shears to make four clean cuts reaching three-quarters of the way down the first can. This will be the bottom (outside) can. The four cuts will form four rectangular portions.

2

Make two cuts at an angle, forming a triangular point at each rectangle. Do this to all the rectangles of the bottom can to form petal shapes.

3

With the needle-nose pliers, carefully bend back the triangles to create petals. (The pliers may make marks on the can, but don't worry—this sim-

ply adds to the charm of the design!)

4

Insert the second can into the bottom can. If it doesn't fit easily inside the outer can, bend down the petals to allow more room. Repeat steps 1 through 3 for the second can, cutting only halfway down the can. These petals will be higher than the first, once you bend them back with the pliers. Pull the second can out of the first can.

5

Apply surface conditioner to each can before painting. Let dry.

6

Paint the sides, top, and bottom of the petals yellow. Paint the inside of each can ocher, and blend ocher onto the sides of the petals to create visual depth. Paint the petal shapes in green at the bottom of the can. Blend green and yellow paint and accent around each petal.

7

When the paint has dried completely, apply the glaze to all painted areas. Let the cans dry completely.

8

Apply glue to the bottom of the second (inner) can and place it into the first (outer) can. Set a heavy object inside the second can until the glue has dried.

9

After the glue has dried, remove the weight, and glue in a glass votive cup. Insert the candle.

FRINGED DAISY CANDLEHOLDERS

10

To make the daisy candle holder, cut eight slices, $1/2$ inch (1.3 cm) deep, in the side of the remaining tin can. Gently bend each slice back (these are your petals).

11

Apply surface conditioner to all areas of the can that will be painted.

12

Paint the petals and the inside of the can fuchsia. Blend medium and light pink paint and apply it to the tips of the petals. Let dry completely.

13

Paint large green triangles around the bottom of the can. Blend green and yellow paint to accent each petal. Let dry completely.

14.

Apply glaze to the painted areas, and let it dry.

15

Glue in a votive cup and insert the candle.

Southwestern Candleholder and Cactus Centerpiece

When the candles are lit, this delightful centerpiece glows like a tiny desert under a full southwestern moon.

DESIGNER
SHELLEY LOWELL

WHAT YOU NEED

3 terra-cotta flower pots, about 3 inches (7.5 cm) wide at the top

10-inch (25 cm) wide terra-cotta saucer

Pencil

Acrylic paints: blue, yellow, peach, and lavender

Paintbrushes, ½ and ¼ inch (1.3 and .6 cm) wide

Water-based polyurethane

Sand, pebbles, or small dried white beans

3 to 4 small cacti

3 white votive candles or tealights

WHAT YOU DO

1

Using the photo as a guide, outline in pencil on the three clay pots and saucer the areas you will be painting. The design featured here captures the shapes of sand dunes and the pinpoint lights of a starry night. Feel free to create your own design.

2

Paint the outside of the pots and saucer, and let them dry for one to two days.

3

Coat the outside of the painted pots and the inside and outside of the painted saucer with polyurethane. (You don't have to coat the bottom of the saucer.)

4

Pour sand or another suitable material into the saucer, up to the edge of the design.

5

Place the candles in the pots.

6

Arrange the candleholders and the cacti in the saucer.

All Souls' Day at the Cochiti Pueblo

In the modern world of light switches and batteries, candles often serve as miniature torches to light our way only when the electricity fails, and we can't find the flashlight. For some cultures, however, these small bearers of flame continue to illuminate a sacred path, providing markers to guide spirits of the dead returning from the world beyond. Such is the role of candles in the All Souls' Day traditions of the Cochiti Pueblo Native Americans.

Although the Cochiti Pueblo Native Americans were converted to Catholicism by the Spanish in the 17th century, for them, November 2 bears the name, "Their Grandfathers Arrive from the West Feast," or, "Their Grandfathers Arrive from the Dead Feast." Occupying the northernmost pueblo among the Keresan-speaking villages of the Rio Grande River west of Santa Fe, New Mexico, this village of Native Americans views All Souls' Day as an opportunity to convince visiting spirits of the dead that they have not been forgotten, and to reassure them that their remaining kin are doing well in the world.

Each family observes the holiday by fasting, and setting out bowls of food for the dead in the corners of their houses.

They leave the doors of the houses open for the returning spirits, and openly display their material goods upon the walls. Finally, candles are lit so that the dead can find their way to their former homes. At nightfall, the men of the village congregate in a ceremonial chamber known as the kiva, where they spend the night singing and slicing up small bits of food as offerings for the returning spirits of the dead.

"Neither do men light a candle, and put it under a bushel, but on a candlestick and it giveth light unto all that are in the house."
— Matthew 5:15

PAPER, FABRIC & BAMBOO

These beautiful candleholders are simple to make by wrapping bamboo place mats around glass jars, and tying them in place with raffia. Set a votive candle or tealight inside the glass, and enjoy the gentle glow.

DECOUPAGE TUMBLERS

Sewing patterns make a great embellishment for heavy glass tumblers. When candlelight shines through the translucent paper, the details of the pattern stand out in a striking way.

DESIGNER
ELLEN ZAHOREC

WHAT YOU NEED

Several large drinking glasses

Old sewing patterns

Polyurethane acrylic gloss

Paintbrush

Scissors

Votive candles

WHAT YOU DO

1

Cut or tear the sewing patterns into small pieces.

2

Apply a layer of polyurethane acrylic all over the outside of the glass.

3

Place a layer of sewing pattern pieces on the sticky surface. Then brush on another coat of polyurethane acrylic. Place another layer of sewing pattern pieces on the sticky surface. Continue in this way until you have added three layers.

4

Finish with a final coat of polyurethane acrylic, and let the decoupage dry.

"Night's candles are burnt out, and jocund day Stands tiptoe on the misty mountaintops."
—William Shakespeare, *Romeo and Juliet*

LEAF CANDLESTICKS

These lovely candlesticks look like they've just walked out of a 17th-century Dutch still life. Add them to your table to create a rich and elegant tableau.

DESIGNER
ANNE MCCLOSKEY

WHAT YOU NEED

2 yards (1.8 m) of muslin

Large bottle of fabric stiffener

Sealable plastic freezer bags

2 glass vases, 8½ inches (21.3 cm) tall

Large plastic trash bags

Plastic gloves

2 flat, small brass candle cups

Acrylic paints: dark brown, dark green, yellow-green, ocher, coral, chocolate, and antique gold

Sponge

Acrylic gloss varnish

Paintbrush

Silk or live leaves to trace

2 cookie sheets

Plastic wrap

Narrow masking tape

Aluminum foil

Heavy floral wire

Cyanoacrylate glue

26-gauge wire

Pencil

2 candles, 12 inches (30 cm) tall

Scissors

Wire cutters

WHAT YOU DO

Making the Bases

1

Cut one yard of the muslin into 2- x 36-inch (5 x 90 cm) strips.

2

Pour a generous amount of fabric stiffener into a sealable plastic bag. Lay the bag flat and add the muslin strips to it, moving them around until they're saturated.

3

Place both vases on a flat work surface on top of a large plastic trash bag. Wearing the plastic gloves, start from the bottom of one vase and wrap the fabric strips tightly around it, overlapping the fabric with every turn around the vase. Keep wrapping and smoothing the fabric until you reach the top of the vase. Tuck the inside edges into the top of the vase, and smooth the lower edges around the bottom of the vase. Repeat the process with the second vase.

4

Cut out four 3-inch (7.5 cm) diameter circles from the remaining yard of muslin, two circles for each vase.

5

Coat two of the circles with fabric stiffener and smooth them together to form one circle. Insert this circle about 1½ inches (3.8 cm) down into the vase opening, smoothing it against the edges. Repeat this step for the second vase.

6

Place one brass candle cup on the muslin insert and gently

flatten it down, then remove the candle cup. This will make an impression in the muslin while it's still wet. Repeat for the second vase. TIP: To speed drying time, place the vases on heating vents or outside if the weather is warm. They may take several hours to dry completely.

7

Paint both vases (including the inside of the vase openings) dark brown, using the sponge. Let dry completely.

8

Lightly sponge on the other colors, allowing some of each color to show through. Don't worry if a little muslin shows through—it will add to the texture of the vases. Let the paint dry completely.

9

Apply a coat of acrylic gloss varnish, and let dry.

Making the Leaves

10

Trace six leaf patterns on the remaining muslin. Double the fabric and cut out each pattern so that you end up with two identical copies of each leaf.

11

Place two leaves at a time in the small plastic bag with fabric stiffener. Once coated,

smooth the edges together to form one leaf. You will have six leaves total.

12

Cover the cookie sheets with plastic wrap and secure with masking tape. Lay out each leaf separately on the plastic-covered cookie sheets. Scrunch up pieces of aluminum foil and place them randomly beneath the leaves. Pinch the leaves to create fabric folds, and pinch the leaf ends into a pleat. Dry the leaves overnight or until they are very dry and stiff.

13

Sponge paint each leaf dark brown front and back, then add a hint of the other colors. Let dry; then apply acrylic gloss varnish to both sides of each leaf. Let dry.

14

Cut three 18-inch (45 cm) pieces of heavy floral wire. Place them side by side and wrap masking tape around them to form one wire.

15

Bend the wrapped wire into a circle large enough to slip easily over the top of one of the vases. Bind the wire securely with masking tape

where the loose ends cross around the neck of the vase.

16

Glue each of the loose ends to the back of a leaf, securing them with masking tape on the back of each leaf if necessary. The stems should run at least 2 inches (5 cm) up the back of the leaf to provide steady support.

17

Cut three 4-inch (10 cm) lengths of heavy floral wire, and wrap them together with masking tape to form a third stem. Glue half of this length of wire to the back of one leaf, leaving the rest of the wire extending from the stem of the leaf. Let the glue dry. Repeat steps 14 through 16 on the other vase.

18

Paint the wire circles and stems as desired. Let dry.

19

Use 26-gauge wire to bind each of the loose leaves to one side of each wire circle.

20

Cut six 8- to 10-inch (20 to 25 cm) lengths of heavy floral wire. Wrap each length around a pencil to create a spiral.

Secure three of the spiral wires to a wire circle by sticking them into the masking tape. Position them between the leaves, using extra thin wire to secure them, if necessary. Repeat on the other vase. These wires and the leaves and stems will remain bendable to style as desired.

21

Dab the spiral wires and any exposed wires with brown paint. Let dry.

22

Using the cyanoacrylate glue, glue the brass candle cups into the center of the impression in the muslin on the inside of the vase openings. Place the candles in the candle cups.

St. Lucia Day

What better place for the Queen of Light to pay a mid-December visit than Sweden, where winter brings long, dark nights and short, gray days? Lucky for the Swedes, St. Lucia, Queen of Light, makes the rounds every year on December 13, in the form of the eldest daughter of each household.

Dressed in a white robe and red sash, the "Lucia bride" wears a crown of ligonberry leaves festooned with lit candles, the hallmark of St. Lucia, whose name stems from the Latin root, luc, meaning "light." Also clad in white robes, the younger girls don tinsel halos, while their brothers, known as star boys, or starngossar, appear in tall cone hats of silver paper and carry star-topped scepters. The party of white-robed children makes its way through the house led by the Lucia bride, who carries a tray of coffee and special saffron buns or ginger cookies, to entice each member of the family from sleep.

While the traditional Swedish celebration of St. Lucia Dagen may be the most distinctive and well-known, Finland, Hungary, Italy, and the Caribbean island of St. Lucia also engage in various customs to commemorate the day.

The origins of the holiday date to the 3rd century A.D., when St. Lucia, born in Syracuse, Sicily, became a martyr for her Christian faith. A nobleman, captivated by her beauty, was promised her hand in marriage. Lucia, a devout Christian, refused to marry the pagan suitor, and took drastic measures to thwart the arrangement. After her husband-to-be claimed that her eyes "haunted him day and night," Lucia reportedly cut out her eyeballs. God restored her eyes as a reward for her sacrifice, and Lucia became the patron saint of the blind. She also came to symbolize the preciousness of light through her act, since she blinded herself on December 13, the shortest and darkest day of the year in the old calendar.

105

LUMINARIAS

This variation of the traditional Mexican paper lantern is a real knockout. The design produces a soft, warm glow that you can sit back and safely admire.

DESIGNER
HEATHER SMITH

WHAT YOU NEED

(for each luminaria)

Glass votive holder and candle

¼-inch (.6 cm) metal hardware cloth*

Assorted sheets of translucent, handmade paper

Spray adhesive

Ruler

Scissors

*available in rolls at building-supply outlets

WHAT YOU DO

1

Decide how wide and tall you would like the finished luminaria to be. Allow for at least 2 inches (5 cm) between the sides of the votive and each wall of the candleholder. Multiply the width of one side by four, add an extra ½ inch (1.3 cm) to overlap the ends, and measure this distance across the metal cloth. Measure and note the height on the cloth to form a long rectangle. Cut out the measured rectangle with scissors.

2

Subtract ½ inch (1.3 cm) from one end of the rectangle and divide the rest into equal quarters. Fold the rectangle at each quarter mark to form an upright cube. Bend the extra ½ inch (1.3 cm) of metal over the adjacent edge to close the cube. The top and bottom of the cube should be open.

3

Hold the handmade paper up to a lamp or window to make sure it's thin enough to allow light to pass through it. Measure enough paper to cover the cube, including an extra ½ inch (1.3 cm) along the top, bottom, and one edge to overlap the frame. Cut out the paper.

4

Spray the metal frame with the adhesive and fold the paper around each side, smoothing it with a firm hand as you go. You should have a seam where the paper overlaps; spray a bit more glue here and press firmly. Fold the extra paper over at the top and bottom of the cube to create neat borders around the openings.

5

Place the luminaria over a votive holder. TIP: When in use, be sure the candle is set in a holder in the center of the luminaria so that there is at least 2 inches (5 cm) between it and each of the paper walls.

Oriental Wrapped Candle

Simple to make and pleasing to the eye, this candleholder pairs handmade Oriental rice paper with a Chinese coin to create an elegant effect.

DESIGNER
SUSAN KINNEY

What You Need

Pillar candle in color of your choice

1 sheet of Oriental rice paper, about 12 inches (30 cm) square

Craft glue

1 piece of raffia, about 20 inches (50 cm) long

1 or 2 Chinese coins or flat, brass beads

Scissors

What You Do

1

Wrap the paper around the candle to create a pleasing-looking sleeve that covers about half of the candle. Trim the paper as necessary, and glue it together.

2

Tie the raffia around the paper, slip on the coins or beads, and tie the raffia to hold them in place. Trim the raffia as necessary.

TIP: As the candle burns down, you'll need to pay attention to the position of the paper to make sure it doesn't come in contact with the flame. You can roll the paper down to shorten the sleeve as needed.

Tips for Storing and Burning Candles

Never leave a burning candle unattended.

Keep lighted candles out of the reach of children and pets, and warn curious little ones about the dangers of fire.

Do not burn candles around combustible materials or when you are using flammable sprays. A can of furniture polish will become a flame thrower when its spray crosses a candle's flame.

Keep an eye on curtains and other items that hang above the candles in your home. The constant heat from a candle's flame may eventually singe fabric and damage other surrounding materials.

If the candles you are using are not specified as "dripless," then be prepared to scrape trails of wax off your candleholders after each use.

Candles keep best when stored in a cool, dark, and

dry place. Wrap candles in paper or cloth, and lay them flat in a drawer or box to prevent warping.

Refrigerated candles, wrapped in foil or plastic to keep the wick dry, burn more slowly than those left at room temperature.

To preserve the shape of a new pillar or hurricane candle, light the new candle and extinguish the flame a few minutes after burning. Pour out the melted wax to create a neat well in the center of the candle; then relight.

Candles burn more evenly and slowly when their wicks are kept trimmed to a ½-inch (1.3 cm) length for tapers and a ¼-inch (.6 cm) length for pillars and votives.

When the wick on a pillar or votive candle becomes buried in wax, use a knife to dig out the wick, then slice a ¼-inch (.6 cm) layer off the top of the candle so it will burn normally. Save the layer of cut wax for making your own candles.

We affixed an assortment of tapers onto slabs of marble and slate using tacky wax, and the result is simply stunning.

Cut-Paper Shades

Underneath the glamorous exterior is an ordinary glass jar. You can use any kind of decorative paper to create beautiful paper shades with simple cutouts that let the candlelight shine through.

DESIGNER:
TERRY TAYLOR

WHAT YOU NEED

Straight-sided glass jars

Typing paper or other scrap paper

Painter's masking tape

Heavyweight paper (watercolor paper, construction paper, handmade paper)

Coins, lids, simple stencil patterns

Sharpened pencil

Ruler

Calculator (if your math skills are rusty!)

Paper punches (optional)

Craft knife with assortment of blades

Self-healing cutting mat or other suitable cutting surface

Bone folder or empty ball point pen for scoring paper

Hot-glue gun or rubber cement

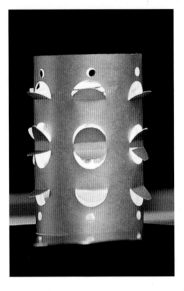

WHAT YOU DO

1

It's helpful to measure, cut, and wrap your jar with scrap paper before you start working with your selected covering; it will save you time and give you a template if you are going to cover a multitude of jars. Follow the directions below using scrap paper, make necessary adjustments, and then work with your selected covering paper.

2

To determine the length of paper you will need to wrap around your jar, measure the diameter of the jar with your ruler. Round your measurement up; for instance, if your jar measures 3³⁄16 inches (8 cm), round it up and convert to an equivalent decimal, 3.25. Multiply the diameter by

pi (3.14). Add an extra ¼ to ½ inch (.6 to 1.3 cm) to this number and you'll have the length you will need to wrap around the jar, including an overlap for gluing. Smaller jars need a smaller overlap, larger jars more overlap.

3

Measure the height of your jar. Add an extra ¼ to ¾ (.6 to 1.3 cm) inch to the height. Smaller jars will need the smaller amount of extra height and larger jars will need more height.

4

Wrap your paper around your selected jar. Secure the overlap with painter's masking tape. Is there enough overlap and is the height to your liking? If not, add length and height to your shade pattern measurements before proceeding with your selected paper.

5

When you're satisfied with the size of your pattern, select the motifs you wish to cut into the paper. Trace coins, jar lids, or simple stencils onto the shade pattern paper where you want the cutouts to be. Wrap your pattern around the jar. Adjust your sketched motifs as desired. You could also use an office hole punch or any of the many craft punches available

on the market to pierce the paper. This would be a really quick and easy way to decorate your shade.

6

Using a sharp blade in your craft knife, practice cutting and scoring your motif. If you used a star: cut the points almost to where they join, score to make a small triangle, and then fold out from the jar. Repeat for the remaining points of the star. When you're comfortable making cutouts on the shade pattern, you're ready to cut out the decorative paper.

7

Using your selected paper, measure and cut the appropriate size for your jar. Use the ruler to guide your knife, and work on a self-healing cutting mat.

8

Lightly pencil your motifs on the wrong side of the paper. Cut and score your motifs from this side.

9

When you have finished cutting and scoring the motifs, wrap your shade around the jar. Lightly mark the area to overlap with your pencil. Hot-glue the overlap, or, for a more permanent bond, coat both sides of the overlap with rubber cement; allow to dry before joining the overlap.

ONE OF A KIND.

We chose colorful bell peppers to serve as candleholders for a south-of-the-border centerpiece. You can turn any number of vegetables into appetizing candleholders, from eggplants to artichokes.

UNIQUE

GOURD HOLDER WITH BRASS BEAD

This stunning candleholder, made from a humble gourd, is small in stature but regal in presence.

DESIGNER
GINGER SUMMIT

WHAT YOU NEED

Bottle gourd, cured and clean*

Metal spoon

Sandpaper

Leather dye, cordovan color

Paintbrush

Wax or varnish

Leather thong

Brass bead

Pillar candle

Saw or power hand-cutting tool

*Gourds can be grown from seed or purchased from garden stores and farmers' markets. Ginger Summit's book *The Complete Book of Gourd Craft* (Lark Books, 1996) features a source list for purchasing seeds and gourds, as well as instructions for growing gourds and decorating them.

WHAT YOU DO

1

Select a bottle gourd with a narrow waist and two bulbs of approximately the same size. Cut off both ends of the gourd, leaving just the middle section, with flares extending from both sides of the waist.

2

Clean the interior of the gourd with the spoon.

3

Sand the cut edges and the interior surfaces.

4

Dye both the interior and the exterior surfaces of the gourd. Let dry.

5

Wax or varnish the entire gourd, and let dry.

6

Wrap a leather thong around the waist of the gourd, and secure it with a bead.

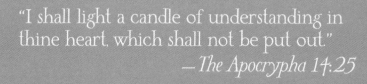

"I shall light a candle of understanding in thine heart, which shall not be put out."
—*The Apocrypha 14:25*

RUBBER STAMP HOLDER CANDELABRA

The designer had a lot of fun transforming an old brass rubber stamp holder into a carnival-colored candelabra.

DESIGNER:
SHELLEY LOWELL

WHAT YOU NEED

Old brass rubber stamp holder*

5 decorative candle caps with polished-brass finish**

Base coat of paint for use on metal

Paintbrushes

Acrylic paints in several bright colors

Small sponge brush

Water-based polyurethane

5 nickels

5 dripless tapers in bright colors

*search flea markets and antique malls

**sold at home-improvement stores

WHAT YOU DO

1

Paint all the metal parts with base paint, including the outside of the candle caps. Let dry.

2

Insert the candle caps into every other holder.

3

Paint whatever design you like, using the paintbrushes and the sponge brush. This is totally free play. Let the paint dry for two to three days.

4

Coat the entire candelabra with polyurethane. Let dry.

5

Put a nickel in each candle cap to create a bottom for the candles to sit in.

MARDI GRAS HOLDERS

These festive candleholders are the perfect size for large pillar candles or votive holders. The designer painted display pedestals using neon-bright markers, and the result is sure to put everyone in the mood to party!

DESIGNER:
ELLEN ZAHOREC

WHAT YOU NEED

Display pedestals*

Enamel paint markers in bright
   colors

Fine-tipped paintbrushes

   *sold at most craft-supply
   and Oriental import stores

Pillar candles

WHAT YOU DO

1

Use simple brush strokes to create bold, abstract patterns with the paint markers. TIP: Be sure to work in a well-ventilated area; these markers are toxic.

2

Let the pedestals dry thoroughly.

DESERT CANDLESTICK

This designer really took a big plunge to create this southwestern candlestick! She chose a new drain plunger because it tickled her funny bone. The miracle is that she made it look like the ceramic work she takes so seriously.

DESIGNER:
PAMELLA WILSON

WHAT YOU NEED

5 wooden cacti*

Acrylic spray paint: off-white, yellow, red, blue, and green

New rubber drain plunger

Dull knife

Hot-glue gun and glue sticks

Taper candle

*available in craft-supply stores

WHAT YOU DO

1
Spray the wooden cacti green, and let dry.

2
Spray the outside of the plunger off-white, and let dry.

3
Spray a light mist of yellow paint on the upper portion of the plunger.

4
Spray a light mist of blue and red toward the top of the plunger to create a sunset.

5
While the paint is still wet, use a dull knife to draw lines around the plunger to create mountains.

6
When the paint has dried, glue on the cacti.

Candlemas

Most people have no idea where the Christian blessing of the candles dwells on the calendar, but they could probably tell you on what month the groundhog comes out of his hole to look for his shadow. Surprisingly enough, these very different rituals celebrate the same date— February 2, or Candlemas.

How did the unique Groundhog Day tradition arise, and why does it take place on Candlemas? Christians have long observed February 2 as a significant religious holiday commemorating the purification of the Virgin Mary in the West and the presentation of Christ in the Temple in the East. The Christian blessing of the candles, the ritual responsible for the holiday's name, did not arise until the 11th century A.D. In Europe, this church-bound ceremony of wax and wick often took place in conjunction with pagan candle-light processions intended to rejuvenate the fields before the planting season. Candlelight was associated with fertility, and with the sun's power, while darkness represented sterility.

In addition to the rituals that took place by candlelight, daylight conventions played a tremendous role in the date's significance: If the sun shone brightly on Candlemas, people knew they were in for more months of snow and cold weather; if Candlemas came with snow and wind, observers were happy—sunshine and warm weather were on the way.

People have long chosen to predict the weather by observing their animal cousins. In America, the groundhog is said to emerge from his hibernation on Candlemas to look for his shadow. If he sees it, he will return to his burrow for six more weeks to remain warm and dry during the promised cold weather; if he does not see his shadow, the groundhog knows spring will arrive soon. The badger has become the trusted Candlemas weather forecaster in Germany, while people in England and France rely on the bear.

These rhymes can help you remember how to interpret the weather predictions cast on Candlemas:

"As far as the sun shines out on Candlemas Day,

So far will snow blow in before May.

As far as the snow blows in on Candlemas Day,

So far will the sun shine out before May."

"If Candlemas be fair and clear,

There'll be two winters in the year."

"If the sun shines on Candlemas Day,

Half the fuel and half the hay."

We filled a pretty glass bowl with polished stones. Then we added a few tealights and votives to create the mood of a miniature rock garden.

INFINITE WISHES CANDLEHOLDER

This delightful clay candleholder makes a perfect birthday gift. Give it to a cherished friend or family member and help celebrate the event with a box full of candles.

DESIGNER:
SHEILA SHEPPARD

WHAT YOU NEED

Pre-made paper mache box with lid, approx. 1 x 3½ x 2½ inch (2.5 to 8.8 x 6.3 cm) *

Pencil

Polymer clay in assorted bright colors

Tools that punch out small stars and hearts*

1 metal bottle cap

Surgical mask

Translucent iridescent powder

Dusting brush for powders (optional)

Parchment paper

Baking dish

1 piece of 12-gauge copper wire, 7 inches (17.5 cm) long

1 metal dowel, ¼ inch (.6 cm) diameter

Cyanoacrylate glue

Acrylic paint in bright colors

Paintbrush

Birthday candles in bright colors

Needle tool

Pasta machine or rolling pin

Slicing blade

Oven

Pliers

File

*available at craft-supply stores

WHAT YOU DO

1

With the lid on the box, use the pencil to mark a line on the side of the box where the edge of the lid rests when it is fully closed.

2

Using the needle tool, lightly scratch up the outside of the box everywhere except for the part above the pencil line. This helps the polymer clay stick to the box.

3

Condition your clay colors and then roll them through the pasta machine on the #4 setting, or use the rolling pin to flatten the clay so it's of medium thickness.

4

Decide where you want the base colors of clay to be on your box; they will form the background for your decorations. Then use the box itself as a pattern to lay on top of your rolled clay sheets. Cut around the box using the slicing blade. Apply the sheets to the surface of the box in your chosen design. Make sure to press all surfaces so they adhere well to the box, and remember not to add clay above the penciled line, or the lid won't fit! Check from time to time during the design process to make sure the lid still fits, especially before you bake the box.

5

Punch out a few stars and hearts from the clay scraps. Embellish the box surface with these heart and star shapes, as well as color strips, and multi-color twists. Be sure to leave enough space in the center of the lid to add your candleholder pedestal.

6

Cover the outside and inside lip of your bottle cap with clay. Form a ¾-inch (1.9 cm) square of clay in a contrasting color, and attach it to the bottom of the covered bottle cap. Attach this to the center of your box lid, clay on clay. Make sure everything is square, and embellish the pedestal as you like, or use the photo as a guide.

7

For the legs, make four 1-inch (2.5 cm) balls of multi-color clay, twisted and secured to the four corners of the box bottom. The legs should stand about ¾ inch (1.9 cm) high. Check to make sure that they are level on all sides.

8

Put on the surgical mask and dust the box with the translucent iridescent powder, using the dusting brush if desired.

9

Place the box and lid separately in a parchment lined baking dish, and bake according to the clay manufacturer's instructions. Allow the pieces to cool completely, and check the lid fit.

10

Using the pliers, wrap the copper wire around the metal dowel to fashion a ¾-inch (1.9 cm) high coil. File the bottom of the coil flat, and use the cyanoacrylate glue to secure it to the center of the bottle cap. Let dry for at least one hour.

11

Paint the inside of the box bottom and outer lip with a brightly colored acrylic paint, and let dry.

12

Fill the box with birthday candles. Insert one candle into the copper coil, light it, and make your wishes!

PRIMITIVE CANDLESTICKS

Gourds are a natural for holding candles. This striking pair echoes the art of many cultures that, for centuries, have used gourds for ceremonies and sacred rituals.

DESIGNER:
GINGER SUMMIT

WHAT YOU NEED

2 small bottle gourds, cured and clean*

Metal spoon

Sandpaper

Black leather dye

Acrylic paint, metallic bronze

Paintbrush

Black paint pen

Wax or varnish

Thin, copper-colored cording

Flat or taper candles

Saw or power hand-cutting tool

Woodburning tool

*Gourds can be grown from seed or purchased from garden stores and farmers' markets. Ginger Summit's book *The Complete Book of Gourd Craft* (Lark Books, 1996) features a source list for purchasing seeds and gourds, as well as instructions for growing gourds and decorating them.

WHAT YOU DO

1
Select two bottle gourds of about the same size and shape. The top bulb should be smaller than the bottom. Cut off the larger bulb end to create the base of the candlestick, making sure the gourd will stand straight.

2
Cut the top off the smaller bulb end so that the opening is about the same diameter as an average candle. TIP: If the opening is too large, you can use a brass candle cup to make it fit a standard candle.

3
Clean out the interior of the gourds using the spoon.

4
Sand the cut edges and the interior of the gourds.

5
Use the woodburning tool to carve simple geometric designs in the base of the candlesticks.

6
Apply a coat of black leather dye, covering the entire gourd, inside and out. Let dry.

7
Paint the base of the candlesticks with a light coat of metallic bronze paint, and let dry. Don't try to cover up all the leather dye; some black showing through adds to the desired effect.

8
Use the black paint pen to outline the woodburned lines.

9
Apply a coat of wax or varnish and let dry.

10
Wrap the copper cording around the gourds' waists.

Contributing Designers

PAMELA BROWN is a professional candlemaker who owns and operates Mountain Lights, a candle and lighting shop in Asheville, North Carolina. In addition to her line of hand-dipped candles, she creates candleholders made from found objects.

ROBIN CLARK and his wife, Helen, own Robin's Wood Ltd., in Asheville, North Carolina, where they manufacture outdoor products for people and wildlife. Robin enjoys trying his hand at other woodworking projects.

PERRI CRUTCHER, for years a professional floral designer and stylist in Paris and New York City, produces elegant floral creations at Perri, Ltd., his equally elegant floral decor studio in Asheville, North Carolina.

MARGARET DAHM lives in Asheville, North Carolina, where she runs a typesetting business with her husband and works as a freelance illustrator. When she's not hard at work, Margaret spends her free time in her garden with her dog and her two children.

MAUREEN (CHA CHA) DONAHUE is a graphic artist who lives and works in Asheville, North Carolina. She has always been very creative, and makes all types of craft projects.

SHEILA ENNIS is a writer and artist living in Boston, Massachusetts. She teaches writing at a local community college and has a small business as a decorative paint finisher. She applies her enthusiasm for crafts to anything that involves paints.

MAGGIE JONES teaches art and photography at Greer High School in Greer, South Carolina. She is the mother of one teenager, one college-ager, four middle-aged cats, five goldfish, and one parakeet. In her spare time between feedings, she enjoys reading, walking, and getting creative with ordinary household objects.

MAX KELLER is a child at heart who continues to fly kites and play in the outdoors. Between studying for classes and entertaining children at an after-school program, Max plays guitar, kicks soccer balls, snaps pictures, and hikes the mountains around his home in western North Carolina.

SUSAN KINNEY is a designer specializing in eclectic interiors, glass and clay jewelry, fabric and rug design, and computer-generated artwork. She attributes the Oriental influence in many of her designs to her years living in Japan and Hawaii. She can be reached at her interior design business, Suezen Designs, in Asheville, North Carolina, at designdr@mind-spring.com.

SUSAN KIEFFER is a former women's clothing designer, travel newswriter, and television camerawoman. She has dabbled in crafts all of her life, and currently works for Lark Books Catalog. She lived in the Florida Keys for many years, but traded the sea for the mountains of Asheville, North Carolina.

LYNN KRUCKE lives in Summerville, South Carolina, with her husband and daughter. She has long been fascinated with handcrafts of all types, and her favorite projects incorporate elements from more than one craft.

DIANA LIGHT, currently residing in Asheville, North Carolina, is an accomplished artisan specializing in painted luminaries and wine glasses. Her delicate images and vibrant colors combine with the translucent properties of glass to create unique objects for everyday use. More of her work can be viewed at www.eden.rutgers.edu/~upchurch.

SHELLEY LOWELL works as a fine artist, illustrator, and graphic designer. She is highly creative in any medium she explores, having won numerous national awards in all of these areas. Her paintings have been exhibited in museums and galleries in New York City, Atlanta, San Francisco, and Asheville, North Carolina. She resides in Arlington, Virginia.

ANNE MCCLOSKEY works in many media and has a fondness for mixing them. She has a tremendous need to create and loves to experiment with new and old materials. She enjoys changing old, flea market items into wonderful new designs. Her work may be found in many books and magazines. Ann lives in Copley, Ohio.

ROB PULLEYN, president of Lark Books, usually is a very hands-off manager. But when the spirit moves him, he can't help using his hands to create projects for our books. He lives in the mountains of western North Carolina.

PAT SCHIEBLE keeps busy with trompe l'oeil and faux finish work for commercial and residential clients in the southeast. Creative and zany ideas spill over into painted furniture, lamps, and candleholders. She lives in Mebane, North Carolina.

SHEILA A. SHEPPARD is a multi-media studio artist who lives in Jonesborough, Tennessee. She loves working with polymer clay because it is a "hybrid of a child of earthen clay and a rainbow." She sells her work throughout the Southeast.

CATHY SMITH is an artist who works in a variety of media. She is currently following her destiny in western North Carolina, encouraged in this pursuit by husband, son, and assorted feline, canine and reptilian family members.

HEATHER SMITH, editorial assistant at Lark Books, grew up on the coast of Maine, where she taught environmental education. She now enjoys crafting, biking, and hiking in the mountains of western North Carolina.

ALLISON STILWELL is a Rhode Island artist who began by working with textiles and making quilts and dolls. She now enjoys working with almost all mediums, creating a wide range of projects.

TRACY PAGE STILWELL creates dolls, quilts, painted furniture, and mixed media projects. She is also known as a teacher, student, and curator, and can often be found in the garden.

GINGER SUMMIT, co-author of *The Complete Book of Gourd Crafts* (Lark Books, 1996) has been fascinated by gourds ever since she retired from teaching seven years ago. She feels passionate about gourds and derives great pleasure from working with them. She lives in Los Altos Hills, California, with her husband Roger.

TERRY TAYLOR is an artist whose work takes many forms, including the pique-assiette technique for making mosaics, beadwork, and one-of-a-kind cards. He lives in Asheville, North Carolina.

COLLEEN WEBSTER earned a BFA degree from the School of Visual Arts in New York City. She currently lives in Asheville, North Carolina.

PAMELLA (WIL) WILSON is an accomplished potter and visual artist whose fine work and gentle personality are celebrated from the Arizona badlands to the North Carolina highlands.

ELLEN ZAHOREC is a mixed-media studio artist, specializing in handmade paper and collage. Her work has been shown internationally and is part of numerous private and corporate collections. She lives in Cincinatti, Ohio.

Contributing Candle Designers and Suppliers

COLONIAL CANDLE OF CAPE COD
P.O. Box 2308
Oshkosh, WI 54903
(800) 932-6733
Website: http://www.blythindustries.com
Wide selection of votives, tealights, tapers, and pillars in an assortment of colors. Call for a retailer in your area.

GUINEVERE'S CANDLEMAKERS
28 N. Lexington Avenue
Asheville, NC 28801
(828) 252-6536
Handmade, molded candles

HEMPHILL CANDLE COMPANY
88 Michigan Avenue
Asheville, NC 28806
(828) 281-1058
Handmade, molded candles scented with essential oils

ILLUMINEE DU MONDE
P.O. Box 304
Bristol, VT 05443
(800) 322-2660
Elegant beeswax candle designs.
Catalog available for retail and wholesale orders.

MOUNTAIN LIGHTS
1 Walnut Street
Asheville, NC 28801
Handmade and specialty candles and unusual candleholders

TWO'S COMPANY, INC.
30 Warren Place
Mount Vernon, NY 10550
(800) 896-7266
Eclectic and unusual candle designs. Call to request a list of retailers in your area.

WAX WARES
12 Riverside Drive
Asheville, NC 28801
(828) 254-7523
Handmade chunk candles

Index

Acknowledgments

I could not have put this book together without the time and talent of a number of people. I would like to thank:

All the designers who contributed projects—their creativity and enthusiasm are boundless.

Sandra Stambaugh, who photographed the candleholders, creating gorgeous, glowing images, and going many, many extra miles.

Dana Irwin, who styled the photographs and designed the book with her great sense of taste and imagination.

The candle companies who donated some of their lovely candles.

The Center for Diversity Education and the Jewish Community Center for loaning us important objects.

Perri Crutcher, Heather Spencer, and Rob Pulleyn, for letting us photograph candleholders in their work places and homes.